Endorsements

"From tragedy to triumph—Fetima's life story, "Eve Before Fruit", is one of perseverance and redemption. Despite numerous unwarranted and unthinkable events that occurred in her life, even beginning at birth, her story will ultimately leave you feeling empowered and hopeful. Fetima's heartfelt passion for the reader to hold onto hope and healing is expressed on every page as she bears her soul. The reader is left knowing no matter what tragedy is experienced on this journey, there is redemption and purpose to be found in pain." — **MJ Nixon**
CEO of Uprooted Heart, Inc

"From the very beginning, you are immediately drawn into the author's world and experiences, in such a way that allows the reader to experience a gambit of emotions. From tears of sorrow, to tears of joy, to shouts of praise and celebration. Fetima makes you feel like she is talking directly to you. An in-depth conversation amongst friends, where she bares the vulnerability of herself, in the rawest form. While Fetima provides us with stories of pain and tragedy, she also provides us with the experiences of redemption, forgiveness, salvation, and triumph. She walks the reader through the journey of forgiveness and healing in such a way that causes self-reflection, so we too can forgive, and we too can be healed from the lingering emotional turmoil." — **Audrey Baker**

"The way Fetima relates her life story is powerful. It shows that God had her in his hands all along. She gives great insight into how God can transform our lives if we allow him. This book has left an indelible mark on my life. This is a life-changing book a must-read. Thanks, Fetima, for being so transparent with your life." — **Charlean Rice**

Eve before FRUIT

AUTOBIOGRAPHY BY
FETIMA S. MCCRAY

MCCRAY BOOKS AND MEDIA

Eve Before Fruit by Fetima S. McCray

McCray Books and Media – Eve Before Fruit

Copyright © 2020 by McCray Books and Media

All scripture quotations are public domain courtesy of Bible Gateway: www.biblegateway.com.

All rights reserved. No part of this book may be reproduced, in any form or by any electronic or mechanical means, including information storage and retrieval systems, photocopying or otherwise without prior written permission from the author(s), except by reviewers, who may quote brief passages in a review or in critical articles.

ISBN# 978-1-7358554-0-0 (physical book)

ISBN# 978-1-7358554-1-7 (e-book)

Library of Congress Control Number: 2020925068

Cover Design by Catherine C. Turner
www.catherinecturner.com

Cover Photography by RJM Photography

Cover Concept and Set Design by Fetima S. McCray

Editing and Layout by LCB Enterprises, LLC
www.consultLatricia.com

Self-Published through McCray Books and Media
www.fetimasmccray.com

Foreword by Sylvia Hayes

PRINTED IN THE U. S. A.

Acknowledgments

To the God that has saved my life, I dedicate mine to You today and always.

To my wonderful husband, thank you for pushing me deeper into my purpose in God, holding up the mirror to my face as God showed me who I am in Him.

To my son, I pray that I make you proud. I cannot wait to see all of the ways that your purpose in God pours out of you.

To my family and friends, thank you for loving me and supporting me in all of my many endeavors.

I love you all dearly.

Dedication

To every woman, and young girl, who has felt trapped in an endless cycle of brokenness, addiction, pain, and self-sabotage, I wrote this book for you.

I want you to know that you can be healed. You can be loved. You can see joy and know inner peace.

What you have experienced does not define you for you are so much more than your wounds.

It is possible to be revived from the ashes of your past pain and trauma and walk in the newness of life.

Let this book show you how.

Table of Contents

Foreword 8

Prologue 10

Chapter 1: Brokenness in the Beginning 12
    The Corruption of Innocence 17
    Mommy Dearest 21

Chapter 2: Who Am I? 31
    Confused and Abused 35
    Deception and Depression 37

Chapter 3: Longing to Belong 43
    The Wounds of the Wolves 45
    A Mosaic of Broken Pieces 56
    From Victim to Vixen 58

Chapter 4: Hearing the Voice of God 68
    Old Body, New Birth 72
    Baptism 77
    The Holy Ghost 80

Chapter 5: Learning to Walk in the New 83
    Healing Hurts 84
    Forgiving the Unforgivable 86
    Forgiving without Apology 88
    Healing Family Ties 93

Chapter 6: Casting Down the Old 97
    Understanding Addiction 98
    Mending the Effects of Childhood Trauma 100
    Sexuality and Self-Worth 106

Chapter 7: God-Ordained Love 112
    Re-Learning Intimacy 114

    Codependency Kills 117

    We Weddy 122

Chapter 8: Life Now and Later **127**

Scripture Glossary **130**

Author's Bio **133**

Let's Connect! **135**

Foreword

It has been said that transparency wins hearts. If one were to take this concept and apply it to the objective of the Christian believer, we would have to agree that transparency wins souls. In order to be an effective Christian – who instinctively captivates a lost soul and enjoins them to follow the path of biblical salvation – one must be willing to altruistically, yet purposefully, reveal how an authentic encounter with Jesus Christ rescued them and what it rescued them from. In her freshman title, Fetima McCray offers a healthy and corroborative contribution to Christian testimonial literature by "shew[ing] forth the praises of Him who hath called [her] out of darkness into His marvellous light" (1 Peter 2:9).

'Eve Before Fruit' is a riveting and poetically eloquent depiction of God's relentless love for His created. McCray's nurturing and selfless approach to authentic transparency allows readers to freely connect emotionally and spiritually through her personal accounts of life, loss, and love. It is through her lived experience that she presents an obvious, providential harmony between the Holy Scriptures and the purpose God places within each of us. In 'Eve Before Fruit,' McCray details the events that divinely ushers her into the Master's arms, resulting in a life-altering transformation.

As you navigate the galvanic waters of this book, I invite you to unlock your heart and immerse yourself in the truth of Christ's love: which is, there is no condemnation in Him and in Him all things become new. I honor Fetima's commitment to painting the picture of this truth through the written work of her journey. I am certain that all who read this captivating narrative will be inspired and empowered. Enjoy.

    Pastor Sylvia E. Hayes, M.A.
    Assistant Pastor, Freedom Church and Ministries, Inc.

Prologue

In my life, I have experienced emotional depths that many could not survive and spiritual height that words cannot express. I have seen immense pain turn the blood of my heart cold, making it septic, and causing me to wonder if I would ever hear the beauty of its rhythmic beat again. My early years were like riding a roller coaster that was diving downward at full speed, barreling headfirst into the earth, with both rickets and bolts shaking frantically. Sometimes I wondered if I would ever survive the ride. But thankfully, that plummeting train fell on new tracks that were laid by the One that had created it.

God redirected the story of my life from being the tale of woman destroyed to the tale of a woman delivered and destined for great purpose. And, I have learned, and am yet learning, that every aspect of my journey—both tragic and triumphant—is crucial to depicting my story accurately. Therefore, I felt it best to share my testimony passionately, in chronological order, ensuring that every phase of freedom is expressed in its fullness. Because of this, there will likely be some parts of this book that might prove difficult to read for some people because of the depth of its content. Some sections may even be triggering, however I've shared openly and transparently throughout this book because I know one key fact: I am not the only person that has experienced what I've lived through. I am not the only one with this story, but I share mine to let the next person know that they are not alone. To let them know that there is there is hope for their future, regardless of what pain they face in their present.

So, though the first few sections may be incredibly sad, please know that the joys of my present condition that I describe in the middle and end of this book are worth reading on for.

I pray that this book plants a seed of faith and curiosity in you that no tactic of the enemy can pluck out. I pray that a seed of hope and faith is planted firmly in the fertile soil of your heart, reminding you that no matter what has happened in your life or family tree, God can STILL bear good fruit there.

Chapter 1: Brokenness in the Beginning

The Bible says that better is the end of a thing than the beginning, and my life certainly seems to hold true to that format. Trauma met me at the very beginning of my life in the loss of my father when I was the tender age of one-year-old. Before I even knew my name, my father was found slain on isolated train tracks in the state of Georgia. He was a long way from Maryland, where he had met my mother, and I was conceived. The story of his death, however, is a bit convoluted depending upon who you ask.

My grandmother, his mother, told me from a young age that he committed suicide. And that's what I believed, and told others, until about the age of 21. This is when I was told by my father's sister that he didn't kill himself, but he was found fatally beaten on those train tracks—cause unknown. My granddad, my father's father, would later tell me his estimation of a cause that I was not prepared for. He told me that my father was murdered in Macon, GA, because he was caught messing around with a Caucasian woman in a place that did not approve of the mixing of colors. I grew weary of asking questions about my dad's death after that. I learned not to dwell on the "how" of my father's passing but to focus only on the "what" that I lost when he left. Variations in stories aside, what one-year-old Fetima lost on that brisk, cold morning was a relationship with the 23-year-old man that held in his hands the keys to her young courage.

I grieved for my father because of who he could have been in my life had he had the opportunity. This may seem subjective, but this is all that I had left of him—my perceptions and hopes of the kind of father that he would have been to me. Though his chair was empty, I respected his place in my heart and never let another man perch there. I've had father figures later in my life, but it always proved too difficult to call them "dad." That spot was reserved for the man that laid with my mother and no one else, because no one else could be Kareem.

My father loved animals, especially cats (and surprisingly enough, so does my husband). My father was a stout man, strong-bodied with round features that would curve into the meekest, most sweetly gentle, smile. The width of his broad shoulders suggested that he could have been a great linebacker and an even better bear-hugger. Those were the shoulders that would have lifted me over his head as he stared up at me beaming in the haloed sun of a careless summer's day. Sometimes, when pictures of my face are taken off-guard, I see his features there. My mocha-hued skin and the concaves of my profile call after a name that I never could. It was as if my father were speaking from within my DNA saying, "You'll always have me here, even though I can never be there." I still wear his features proudly after all these years in remembrance of the man whose life came in and out of the world as a whisper under breath.

I even hold my hands together like he did, which completely blows my mind. There's an almost haunting feeling of nostalgia that comes over you when you realize that something so innate within the memory of your muscles belongs to a person that you know so little about. It's kind of like finding an old jacket in your mother's attic that smells and looks familiar, but you can't, for the life of you, remember why, or how, or who, or when. You just know that for some unknown reason, that musky half-known aroma brings tears to your eyes, and a lump in your throat and a pressing on your chest.

I imagine that, if I was that little girl that found that old attic jacket, I would pull its weight over my fragile shoulders, draping the collar tightly around my neck, and clench the arms of the jacket tightly over my own to mimic the embrace of the man that used to wear it. I'd look up at the sky with teary eyes and wonder if I would ever see my daddy again. Unfortunately for me though, I have no attic jacket. All that I have are aged pictures, an old license, and my imagination to build the memory of a man from the pieces that he left behind.

I remember my dad's mom showing me a picture of my father when I was about eight or nine years old. I was in absolute awe of him—this being the first time that I had ever seen my father's face. This big man with massive arms, posing in front of a tree line. In his hands, as he smiled gingerly, was the body of a small grey kitten. His face was glowing and beaming with pride. It was like looking into another dimension where the man that I had only rarely heard of had not just a face, but a life, and a story, and interests, and someone to give his love to. I remember wishing with all my heart that he could have given the love that he had for that kitten to me. I envied that cat for what it was able to be that I couldn't—immortalized in photographs, tightly held in the arms of my dad. I would have many more somber thoughts like this as I grew into adolescence, and then into adulthood. Each year that went by met me with a deeper longing for the father that I never got to have. There's a different type of grief that occurs when a child loses a parent early on in his or her childhood. When I've spoken to friends who have lost parents in their teenage and adult years, they always talk about how the memories of that parent stir up the grief for them. They talk about how the memories stir when they hear a song that they used to sing with their loved one or visit a restaurant that they used to frequent together. They mention how holidays at home feel bittersweet because they only remind them of who they lost (and sometimes this grief keeps people from even returning home altogether). But, unabashedly, most say that over time, you learn to cherish those grief-stricken memories more than you allow them to cause you pain. The memories become a memorial of happier times, solidified with the gratitude that one was "at least" able to have made them before the parent passed away. But, for the person who has lost their parent(s) as young as I have, grief and the process of healing look much different.

When my father first passed, I had no way of even understanding the concept of death, being far too young to fully ascertain its permanence. Even when I was a bit older and I was told that my father had passed away, the words didn't mean as much to me, because I didn't yet feel that void his death caused in my life. I didn't yet see how my life was different than anyone else's. It wasn't until I saw other young girls madly in love with their fathers that I truly began to miss mine. I missed my father when I had back-to-school nights and didn't have a dad to introduce to my teachers. I missed my father when I heard other children so effortlessly say "my daddy," with a smile and just a hint of glitter in their eye. I missed my father when the first boy broke my heart (and the second, and the third, and the fourth). I missed him when puberty came, and I felt vulnerable and unbeautiful. I missed him when it was time for me to walk down the aisle to my husband. I have been missing him all my life and will likely continue to. Though I had never really known the man to truly miss his presence. I was most saddened by the fact that I would never get the opportunity to experience him enough to miss him and love him like I saw other girls and young women love their dads. I mourned for all the memories that I would never be able to make.

His time on this earth had come and gone, and I missed it. I missed him. This kind of grief is more prolonged than the typical. It deepens as each milestone and major moment is met without the presence of my dad in my life. And though I had tried desperately to supplement fatherly affection and advice, I soon realized the futility of my fight. My father was gone. My relationship to him would only be as deep as my gaze upon the old picture of him holding that young kitten.

There are so many unlearned life lessons that young women miss out on when they don't have a relationship with their father. They miss out on having that stern but trustworthy voice of wisdom that the patriarch of the family brings. They miss out on having that strong male figure to teach them about love and respect and responsibility. This is God's intention for the father in the family structure—to lead the family wisely in His direction, protecting them both naturally and spiritually, loving them, and taking great care in making provision for them. There is a great role that a father plays in the life of his children and especially in the life of his daughter(s). It's a father's duty, and joy, to teach his daughter how to be a confident and grounded beauty—having a firm knowledge of her worth and not allowing it to be tossed to and fro by another man's opinion of it. Fathers show their daughters how a man should treat them, and how a queen should be cared for and respected (this example also begins with how the father treats the mother). Fathers bestow upon their daughters the first remnant of the emotional security that will build the foundation of how they view themselves. They do this by showing their young women that a man can love them, treat them well, honor, and respect them without requiring sex or any other form of currency in return. A lot of women, myself included, would have done well to have learned this lesson calmly in their youth and not through repeated broken hearts.

This is why a young lady's relationship with her father is so particularly important. For if a young lady never learns that compliments and kind words don't directly equate to love, then she is much more likely to trade her sanity and purity for sex with someone who hasn't proven himself and isn't worthy of her. She may trade sex for acceptance. Sex for adoration. Sex for a feeling of belonging. Sex for any feeling at all. In fact, if you look at the broken heart of many women and young girls who are deeply scarred or wounded from their childhood, you might often find the hole where their father should have been. You might see the need for affection and attention—a result of the absence of appropriate male affirmation. You might see the need to be "claimed" by a man or the desperate fear of being without one. You might see that her worth is more so measured by the likes on the screen or the number of suitors available in the DM's (direct messages). And if you take an even deeper look into the wounded heart of a fatherless daughter, you might even find staring back at you the immortalized eyes of the young girl who is still painfully striving to be accepted by her daddy. I don't think we ever fully understand the depth of the root of fatherlessness, as women, until God opens our eyes to it. So many women carry that small, wounded girl with them from year-to-year, never realizing (or even acknowledging) how these wounds show up in the many different areas of their lives. These wounds are made even deeper in a young girl who has also experienced childhood molestation by a trusted older male.

I was such a girl.

The Corruption of Innocence

The man who robbed me of my childhood innocence was, unfortunately, a very trusted family member. The molestation occurred from the ages of four to seven years old and was initially introduced to my tender knowledge as a game. Something so disarming and so minuscule that it wouldn't bear mentioning to my mother or anyone else. This "game" would become the thing that opened my mind and my body to things no child should ever experience. It almost reminds me of the story of Eve and the deceiver, Satan, in the garden of Eden. There was Eve in a land of perfection, with no pain and an abundance of food, flora, and fauna. All she knew was peace, contentment, and wonder. All she knew about the world that she lived in was good. I can imagine her looking at every leaf on every tree in the garden, mesmerized by the veins that carried the nutrients from the branches to the tips of the leaves. I can imagine her frolicking with dangerous animals who knew not yet the lethal power of their jaws and claws. I can see her now with bright eyes, a big smile, and a heart that only knew trust and love. A heart that only knew God and knew good. But the crafty serpent, jaded by the corruption that he had already eaten, tricked young Eve into consuming the forbidden fruit. Now her eyes were opened, and she was able to see the world in a way that she had never seen it before. Where she had only known the beauty of good, now she had learned of the treachery of evil. An evil that would turn the tide of the nature of her life and her family's life, from generation to generation after her. Now evil was staring her right in the face and she realized, all at once, that she was naked. Vulnerable. Fragile. Deceived, robbed, confused, and scared. Eve's life, and the life of everyone attached to her, was never the same after that moment.

The same was with me.

I had trusted in someone whom I believed had my best interest at heart and didn't realize the dangers of what I had experienced until after my eyes had been opened by mom and my therapist. I only learned that what we were "playing" wasn't a game when my mother became aware of it. I can imagine that I felt some of the same feelings that Eve did on that fateful day. Unclean. Naive. Stupid. Dirty. Guilty. Heartbroken and sorrowful. The news ripped through my immediate family unit and all were affected, yet my mother was the one most in pain about it. How could I have known that my agreement to keep the game a secret was me giving someone permission to violate me privately, gaslight me publicly, and corrupt me mentally and emotionally? Just like Eve, my life from that point was forever different. Because of my early proximity to sexual stimulation, I became a very hyper-sexualized child. I didn't understand the proper physical boundaries. I talked about inappropriate things at times, thinking that risky physical touch or sexual suggestions were normal parts of everyday conversations. I became bolder when speaking to adults of the opposite sex and found myself becoming emotionally attached to adults in a way that a child should not. I started to self-pleasure and chase the sensations that I had been exposed to decades before I was supposed to.

There was one time where my mother caught me on the couch in the act (I thought that she was too busy to notice). She walked over to me and pulled back the covers, exposing what I was doing, and all that I could think of was to lie to try and conceal the obvious. I followed suit with what I knew to do—disguise and deflect from what was being done under the covers. My mother put me into therapy shortly after everything came to light, and I truly thank God that she did. Some children don't get that type of support from their parents in these kinds of situations, and it's very unfortunate. Though my sessions were short-lived, there was one house visit that I remember vividly. My therapist was just beginning to explain to me that what my family member did to me was wrong. That was the day that it finally registered in my little heart that I was robbed of something precious. As I pensively played with the clay that my therapist gave me to keep me occupied, she asked me what I would do if that family member ever tried to hurt me again. With new anger in my heart, I looked her square in her eyes, balled my fist up, and smashed my clay flatly with a resonating thud into the table of our dining room. My brokenness had just been realized and resentment and hatred were budding up in me for the very first time.

> **My mother was the one who stood in the gap between me and my abuser.**

Shortly after my therapy began, my healing process was stunted as I lost my hero, best friend, and all sense of stability. My mother was the one who stood in the gap between me and my abuser. My mother was the one that held me tightly together even though I didn't yet understand that I was broken. My mother was the one that took me to therapy to begin the initial steps of my healing process. And then, all of sudden, just as I began to understand enough of my trauma to be filled with rage and guilt, my mother,—the one who knew me best and loved me most— passed away from breast cancer.

I was devastated beyond measure.

What deepened the overall pain of her loss was that I and my brothers had to watch as breast cancer suffocated the beautiful light that made my mother who she was. With eyes blurred by a flurry of tears, we watched the flame of my mother's life dim rapidly into a dull hue before disappearing into a vapor of smoke. It all happened so fast. I learned later that my mother had been fighting cancer for a few years, but early efforts to remove it all had proven unsuccessful. Through countless treatments and chemotherapy, my mother's medical team worked feverishly to cure her before realizing that the cancer was far too advanced to stop. Slowly, she lost her hair and her energy, but never her smile. She was always optimistic even in the face of the direst situations and could find a positive spin to any obstacle that life threw at her. We would have days where we danced and sang songs while trying on her different wigs. We had days where my mom would cook for my brothers and me and days where we binge-watched VHS tapes and ate junk food. But, looking back at it all, I know that through the endless days of fun and laughter, there were still deeper questions and concerns looming over my mother's mind like a swinging guillotine. How can a single mother of four children tell her kids that she's going to die? How does a woman with one deceased baby's father and two absent ones spring up enough future hope within herself to spread amongst the wide eyes of the children that she's nurtured all alone for so many years? How can she look into the eyes of the daughter that looks just like her and tell that child that the clock of her mortality is ticking much faster than the years are going by? Yes, my mother knew full well what she faced as her health options became more and more limited. But I think that the very real prospect of leaving her children behind to scathe such unchartered territory alone is what ultimately hurt her the most.

Mommy Dearest

My beautiful mother was, without a doubt, the sweetest woman that I have ever known and will ever know. She was a hard-working single mother and a woman of faith (A Jehovah's witness that raised us in the same faith—though my father was Muslim). She had the brightest smile and the most exuberant personality, shining a beacon of light in every life that she touched. I have yet to meet a person that truly knew her and didn't remember her fondly.

My mother was a natural nurturer. The kind of mom that could stop young tears effortlessly with just a cheek kiss and a loving smile. She nurtured every dream and aspiration that was shared with her and admonished her children to look both inwardly and toward the heavens. She was a spectacular woman and I find solace in knowing that the woman that I have adored since birth lives healthily in me. I also see her smile in the beaming curves of my lips. I see her joy in my steps as I play with my son and crack jokes with my loved ones. I feel the nature of her warmth in how I love and minister to those that I care about. I have learned to find joy in knowing that even though my parents are gone, it is their DNA that courses through my veins. It is their DNA that makes up the shape of my face and my waist and my eyes and ears. I was crafted from their love for one another and they both live in me. In the case of my mother, what also lives in me are all the memories that I shared with her. Sure, seven years may not seem like much, but I remember my experiences with her vividly because of how she made me feel about myself when I was with her. We shared in her love for musicals and black-and-white movies, things that I still adore to this day. We would watch "Charlie Chaplin and the Eating Machine," or sing along to every song in "The Sound of Music" — twirling around the room together as we yelled about the hills being "alive" and described a few of our "favorite things." Her graceful gait was always met with my clumsy, short-legged shuffle, but we danced together beautifully all the same. We would study excerpts of the Bible together and I would tell her about my wildest dreams and aspirations in the greatest detail that I could utter. My mother, eyes wide with pride and amazement, would listen intently meeting my excitement with her emphatic affirmation. She instilled confidence in me that made me feel like I could change the spin of the Earth on its' axis if so desired. She taught me that I was strong. That I was capable. That I was loved and irreplaceable. Her love for me and my brothers was immeasurable, and we loved her right back with the same fervency. She was my absolute best friend, and there will never be another like her.

Though my mother had a mastectomy, the breast cancer had already migrated further into her body, so chemotherapy was the last treatment resort. Slowly, but surely, she lost weight and became more fatigued throughout the day. The treatment was tough on her body, but the cancer itself proved to be developing more rapidly than the treatment could treat it. She was deteriorating fast and there was nothing that anyone could do to stop it. Our everyday lives changed as we adjusted to life with a mother that was fatally ill. We couldn't twirl around to Sound of Music as much, and our days of play became days of me watching movies alone with her napping on the couch. All the while, she kept a smile. She tried everything in her power to maintain a sense of normalcy for us, but she was getting weaker and weaker and she drew closer to the end of her life.

I remember running up to her one afternoon and trying to shake her awake. My brothers were gone out with their friends that afternoon, and it was only me and my mother in the house. There was something that I wanted to show her, though now I can't remember what it was. I tapped her shoulders and called out to her in excitement, but she wouldn't respond. Confused, and a little fearful, I nudged her more pensively and called out to her yet again to no avail. Futility and panic began to beat in my chest as I screamed for her with my voice cracking and tears flooding my eyes. Lord, please tell me that my mother is alive! As I looked down at my mother, who laid in silence, a thousand thoughts raced through my head. Is my mother dead? This was the question that choked up my chest and brought me to my knees weeping. I grabbed my mother and started to cry loudly, wailing in anguish, because I believed her to be gone. This action was what finally startled my mother awake and she scooped my tiny, tear-filled face into her hands. She asked me what was wrong, and I tried to respond in between the sobs of my delicate heart. I told her that when I couldn't wake her up, I feared that she had died, and I didn't know what to do, because I was all alone.

It was at that moment that I finally felt the weight of my mother's heavy heart grieving for my future. She hugged me tightly as we cried together, reassuring me that she was "here." That moment was an emotional roller coaster for both of us. I went from believing that my mother was dead to knowing that she was alive, and she went from reassuring me that she was alive to fearing the possible reality of me finding her dead. Or at least, that's what I assume she was thinking because shortly after that incident she sent me away to live with some friends of our family.

These were my mother's friends, so I didn't know them well, but she trusted them with me. Their kids were much older than me, so I spent most of my days by myself and missing my family. The mother and father of the family were nice and did everything in their power to keep my mind off of my mother's condition, but at the end of the day, the distance from my mother made me worry about her more. The nicer they were to me the more I wondered if I would ever see my mother again. I could tell that they knew more about her condition than what details they would share with me, but I didn't understand why they wouldn't tell me what they knew. Being an adult now, I realize that they were trying to protect me from things that I couldn't yet understand the gravity of.

I didn't have any real insight into the severity of my mother's condition until we went to visit her in person. Every time we would visit my childhood home my mother would seem sicker and sicker. She looked pale and was constantly nauseous, violently vomiting into heavy-duty garbage bags, barely even able to breathe in between fits. My brothers stayed with my mom to care for her since they were much older, tirelessly cleaning up after her and switching out her bags whenever necessary. Seeing her like that, with her condition worsening more drastically every time, always made me bad for my brothers when I got to leave. I wondered how it felt for them to be the ones in the trenches with my mother as sickness ravaged her body. And honestly, it's something that we still haven't talked about to this day, because I can't imagine how painful those memories must be for them. So, I don't ask about them. I just let the shared grief and pain of missing our mother be unspoken yet understood.

It wasn't too long after my last visit with my mother that she was moved to a hospice. A hospice, for those who don't know, is a place where terminally ill people go to transition into death more comfortably and peacefully. I only got to visit her one time in that hospice, and it is a day that I will never forget until the day I die. It's my assumption now that the hospice had told my family to come and say our "final goodbyes", because I was told that my brothers had just left and that my uncle and my cousins were on their way. I found it weird that we all were trying to visit my mother at one time. After all, I wanted to spend some time alone with her because I missed her so sorely. I was far too young to understand the concept of a "final goodbye" and a part of me knows that's why everyone felt it best to shield me from the true nature of that fateful visit. The other part of me wishes that I would have known more about what was going on, so that I could have been more aware of what I should have been doing or saying or feeling. I just thought that it was another ordinary day.

I walked into the hospice room where my mother laid and saw her hooked up to an array of wires and monitors. I barely recognized her. Her face was much slimmer, she had a breathing tube in her nose and the staff had removed her wig, revealing her smooth, bald head. She didn't look like the mother that I had remembered. I almost, for a second, thought that we were in the wrong room. It was hard to wrap my mind around the fact that the person lying motionless in the bed before me was the same person that spun around with me like Julie Andrews on grassy, green hills until we both were dizzy. She didn't seem like the mother who laughed loudly with me and tickled me into submission. Her face didn't light up with a smile like the sun finally peeking out from behind a cloud on the first day of summer. Its warmth begging you to bask in it and smile back. She didn't radiate life and vibrance like my mother did.

I wondered if she was even my mother at all.

In the sheer shock of the moment, I initially kept my distance from my mother's bed, fearfully cautious of separating my back and palms from the cool of the hospice walls. I looked closely at the woman in the bed again and scanned her face for something–anything familiar. My mother's friend tried to encourage me by saying, "Don't you know who that is? That's your mom. Go say, 'Hi' to your mom!" I could tell that her excitement and smile were both forced, and it made me feel awkward. I hesitated for a breath, still searching for something familiar in the unfamiliar face of the woman in the bed. "She kind of looks like my mother when she's sleeping," I thought to myself. Then, in a burst of faith and courage, I ran to the bed and grabbed the first hand that I saw and held it in my own.

I was immediately taken aback by how icy cold it felt.

I spun around and in my sassiest, yet precocious, little voice I told my mother's friend that they needed to turn the heat up in my mother's room, because 'she's cold.' She quickly touched my mother's hand and rushed me out of the room, gesturing to some of the nursing staff on the way out. She told me to stand over to the side as she spoke to the nurses. A nurse went in to check on my mother and rushed out of the room almost as quickly as she had entered. Moments later a swarm of adults in scrubs bombarded my mother's room with a full crash cart and quickly closed the door behind them. What was that all about? I thought to myself. My mother's friend grabbed my hand and lead me further out into the hall as I wondered if I had said something or done something wrong that caused our visit to be cut short. We walked to her car,

Brokenness in the Beginning

and she told me to wait in the back seat while she went to, "ask about the heat."

As I sat in the back seat of her vehicle another car pulled up behind us. It was my uncle (my mother's brother) and my cousin. As he parked his car, he greeted my mother's friend and walked to her, asking her something that I couldn't quite make out. She responded, and the words hit him in the chest like the pellets of a shotgun. He staggered back and dropped his head, wounded from the blast as he clutched his chest and heaved for breath. My cousin was within earshot and began to scream and cry. What I didn't realize until later was that she had told my family that my mother had passed. As she walked back to the car, I saw her take a deep swallow and try to flash my confused face a half-smile. She got in the driver's seat of the car and began to pull away as my cousin ran behind us crying and reaching out for me. I will never forget that moment. Though I had no clue what had happened I could tell by everyone else's reactions that it was something drastic.

We drove back to the house of our family friend and before we were able to exit the car, she received a phone call. She listened to the person on the other line, let out a large sigh, and said that we needed to make "one more stop." We drove to the house of a couple that my mother was very close to, and we walked inside. There was an unusual feeling in the house this time and every eye looked wet and weary. Another one of my mom's friends was there, and he asked me to come and sit beside him. He took out a children's Bible and asked me if I remembered what happened to Lazarus. I told him, "Yes. Lazarus died." He spoke his next words to me with great sadness.

He said, "That's what happened to your mother."

My head immediately began spinning. Dead?! Like dead and gone and never to return (dissimilar to the story of Lazarus)? How could my mother have been dead when I just saw her?! What does dead mean? Would I never be able to see her face again? Who am I without her? Where will I go? I thought I would be able to go home soon and everything would be like it used to be again. Where is my mother? Sorrow started setting in as I began to realize that everyone was gathered in that house to share with me the news of my mother's passing. She really was gone.

The joyful smile that would greet me in the morning, was gone. The beautiful voice that would sing with me and to me would never call my name again. Those eyes that sparkled like the twinkle of sunlight on the face of winter's lake were now closed and would be closed forever. My mother was gone, and I had never gotten the chance to say goodbye. As heartbreak began to burn through my chest, my eyes darted desperately across the room for a place to hide. The pitiful stares of everyone in the room felt like salt and acid on fresh wounds, and I had to get away from them quickly. I jumped behind the first thing that I saw—the leaning back of an old reclining chair—and sought refuge there. I yanked the chair back as far as it could go down, allowing my body to be as crushed under the cushion as my heart felt. It was there, crawled up into a ball with my head between my knees, that I finally was able to cry like I needed to. It's an isolating pattern that I would keep in the years to come to shield the manifestation of my most broken parts from the faces of others. I cried in loud, inconsolable, guttural sobs. There were no eyes to sting behind that couch, so I cried behind that couch and grieved the loss of the only arms that I had ever truly felt comfort in. I cried there, behind the cushion of that old chair, for what felt like hours. I cried until my head throbbed and I could no longer breathe through my nose or even think straight.

After I finished crying, I sat in silence for a while and tried to muster up enough courage to finally speak on what I was just told. I took a deep breath, pushed the back of the chair into an upright position, and prepared to present myself to the rest of the room. What I didn't know though, was that more family members and family friends had silently crept into the room while I was crying, and now every eye, old and new, was all on me. I shrank instantly. My courageous chest deflated, and I bolted out the open front door. I didn't know where I was going to run or what I was doing, but I had to escape what I was feeling for a moment and running away was the only thing that I could think to do. As I raced down the stairs to the sidewalk, I heard my mother's only sister call out to me. She asked me why I left, and I told her that it was because I was afraid. I was afraid that I was alone and that "nobody would be my family anymore." Now, who was I since my mother was gone? It was my mother who had always affirmed me. It was my mother who had spoken purpose and great conquests over me and loved me unconditionally. My aunt saw my wounded anxiety and reassured me that my family would always be my family, no matter what, and that she would always be there for me. And, to this day, she has never voided that declaration. Though many family members and friends have stepped up to build a family structure around me over the years, they could never fill the void that was left in my life after my mother passed. I have come to realize that once you lose a parent, even both parents, you are ultimately left with a space in your heart that no one else has the capacity to heal or fill but God Himself. And, though that is undoubtedly true, it's still a tough pill to swallow with a lump in your throat.

Eve Before Fruit

"My memories don't do her justice, and all I have is just THIS:
These 5-second, fleeting movies that always seem to move me back to a place where love had a face,
-a home
-a heart
-a time
-a place,
And these memories keep fading, ever slowly, fading away,
I pray they never erase"

– "Mama" Written Oct. 27th, 2010

Chapter 2: Who Am I?

Some weeks after my mother's funeral it was decided that my brothers and I would be split up. It seemed that there was no home that could house all four of us. One brother was sent out of state, one brother was sent to live with his father's side of the family, and one brother was sent elsewhere. I was sent to live with my dad's mom. I didn't know much about her, or my dad's side at all really, but I did remember her visiting my mom's house a few times when I was younger. All in all, though, moving to my grandmother's house was one of the biggest culture shocks of my young life. In many ways she was the total opposite of my mother. My mother warmed the house with affection and allowed room to be silly and have fun, but my grandmother ruled with order and warmed behinds—only making room for what made sense and what would be profitable in the real world. My seven-year-old head that was in the clouds had to learn to come down to earth fast.

> *My sweet soft voice seemed far too fragile now, and that fragility was not celebrated.*

I went from being the youngest and only girl in my immediate family to being the oldest of several girls in my grandmother's house. I went from being the spoiled princess to being the one responsible for many others. My sweet soft voice seemed far too fragile now, and that fragility was not celebrated. My grandmother and I came from two vastly different worlds and that was evident in how we interacted with and often misunderstood one another. My mother was very gentle in how she interacted with me. She took great care in attending to my feelings and hearing me out when I was hurting. My grandmother did not mince her words for anyone, children, animal, or adult, and the sparkles in my eyes didn't change that. My mother spent intentional time with me, actively listening to my wildest dreams and imaginations, no matter how far-fetched or unrealistic they would seem. My grandmother, on the other hand, didn't have the time or the patience to hear things that didn't make sense or weren't logical. She just didn't understand the point of wasting time discussing things that she deemed as unrealistic. Unfortunately, though, emotional imagery and daydreams are what fueled my mind. You could have even called me a flower child. I only wanted to think about what was good, exciting, and full of wonder. My grandmother was only interested in discussing what was useful, responsible, and tangible. We rarely saw eye-to-eye in my younger years, and her brand of "real" love began to slowly chip away at the hopeful lens that I viewed the world by. Looking back on it, I know that she loved me in her way. She just expressed love in a way that was completely foreign to me, and therefore I interpreted this as a complete lack of love. Did she have her flaws as all people do? Absolutely. She was hypercritical, impatient often, quick to make judgments, and even said some terrible things about me, my future, and my mother. It's the truth.

> *" I felt like I was gasping for air and everyone was just watching me suffocate.*

I became much more broken and insecure during my time with my grandmother. I don't think she did any of those things intentionally though, that is, I don't believe that she ever truly set out to hurt me. She was just a woman who had lived her life, raised her children, and was trying to keep me–her granddaughter–out of the foster care system. She had just retired from a successful career and was looking forward to living her years out as she pleased before taking me and my cousins, into her home. I'm sure that was a challenge for her that she did not expect. Additionally, my grandmother was living with her own wounds. After all, she didn't just lose my father (her son), but she had outlived every son that she birthed. My grandmother had five children and by the end of her life, she only had one surviving daughter left. I, in no way, can imagine her pain. She kept it bottled up behind her sternness and rarely spoke explicitly about it. But the pain was there all the same. You could feel it.

I could see it the way that she spoke to me. Her harsh words and stern demeanor were greater indicators of what was going on inside of her own heart and mind rather than simply who she was as a person. My grandmother would say some very hurtful things to me at times, things that I still struggle with dispelling in my mind to this day. She was brass and hypercritical, but she also had great wisdom and insight. She taught me how to be self-sufficient in maintaining a home and how to be financially mindful. She taught me what it means to stand up for yourself though, admittedly, that is still a lesson that I'm learning. She taught me the importance of taking pride in myself and my appearance. She taught that looks weren't everything and that intelligence was key. My grandmother had a huge collection of diverse books, novels, encyclopedias, horror stories, and autobiographies. She would always encourage my cousins and I to read for understanding, read ahead in class and learn to read a room. All in all, I truly do believe that she did her best in raising us. I think she gave us all that she had left to give, honestly, and I have grown to respect her for that and love her more. And yes, I say love. Though my grandmother and I rarely got along (especially in my adolescent years), I still loved her dearly.

Since I knew that I wouldn't receive the kind of affection that my mother gave me from her, I desperately tried to do what I could to coax any affection from her. I tried to do well in school, I read as many books as I could. I would give her compliments every time I thought to, and still my grandmother's affection would not be bought. Nothing that I did was ever to her satisfaction—from the way that I talked, to the way that I breathed to the way that I swept the floor. I was constantly under the microscope and daily unsure of my ability to do anything correctly. I was searching for some positive reassurance that I could understand but the language barrier between how my grandma and I communicated was impossible to break through. My grandmother's rejection of all that I was giving her made me wonder if there was just something fundamentally wrong and unacceptable about me. Was I unlovable? Did I need too much? As my heart rang with more questions than answers, I began to retreat more and more into myself. I felt trapped.

Hers was a world of "yes ma'am" and "no ma'am," switches and belts and no bedtime stories.

Mine was a place of sensitivity and need and raw emotions. It was like mixing oil and water and fire and gasoline. I somehow knew how to effortlessly enrage her, so I walked on eggshells like my feet were made with lead. Every step had to be calculated and every word had to be thought through. I couldn't be my usual self, because that version of me got eaten up and cut down with harsh words and criticisms. Maybe I just wasn't tough enough to keep up with someone like my grandmother. We just didn't gel well, and I was hurting deeply because of it.

I tried to talk to my grandmother about how I was feeling and how her approach made me feel bad, but it only registered with her as being "grown," "disrespectful", and "ungrateful." I would tell her that I felt like a caged bird, and she would tell me to fly away and leave the house if I'm that unhappy. If I told her that I felt unloved, she would get defensive and angry and remind me of all that she's done for me. When, me telling her that I didn't feel loved wasn't an indictment on her ability to care for me financially, it was a probe to discuss how we could better communicate emotionally. I know that a lot of her approach may have been a generational thing but, either way, her responses to me in my rawest moments left me holding the bag of my broken pieces with no one to help me sort through them. With no aid in sight, my grief and depression started to fester more sourly within me. I felt like I was gasping for air and everyone was just watching me suffocate. I was breaking on the inside and I needed someone to truly see me and hear me.

Confused and Abused

To make matters worse I was also fighting a war with another family member who disliked me from the very first moment that I came to live with my grandmother—my aunt. I don't know if it stemmed from disdain for my mother or if there was just something in her that hated the light in me, but she made her distaste for me evident from day one. She would do anything in her power to make me look bad in front of my grandmother or make me feel horrible about myself and my life. She was angry, violent, and untrustworthy, looking to make my life miserable at every turn for her own entertainment. She would put me in situations that a child shouldn't be in, like hanging with her and her friends as they partied, and then accuse me of being "fast" in front of my grandmother. This then validated my grandmother's assumptions that I was "trying to be grown." She would outright lie about things that I "said" and threats that I "made" and then threaten me with bodily harm if I called her a liar. Her emotions were often volatile, swinging from fun aunt to fatal aunt, in a day, a minute or an instant. I might be sharing a laugh with her one moment and then be knocked to the ground the next. She especially watched my relationship with my cousins (her daughters) and my grandmother. If she felt that my grandmother and I had too much peace or contentment in our communication, or if she saw my grandmother complimenting me or being proud of anything that I had done, she would sow seeds of discord to make my grandmother distrust me. She would do the same when she saw the bond that I had with her daughters.

My aunt made me appear to be the enemy that came into the family and disturbed the balance. She made me feel, every day, how out of place I was in her family circle. I was "Cousin It" and "Chocolate Drop"—someone to be laughed at and underestimated at every turn. She would even pit my cousins against me; making up some offensive lie about something that I "said" about them. Those girls and I were like sisters, and she hated to see it. Remember how I said that I was immediately thrust into taking care of other children? My cousins (really, my sisters) were those children. We not only watched TV together, but I helped them with their homework. I washed them up in the mornings and made sure that they were fed before school and had their uniforms on neatly. I would sing them to sleep at night and read them stories from the same books that I loved. Did we fight like sisters sometimes too? Yes, of course. But as much as my aunt tried to make me feel like an outcast, my bond with my cousins remained tight and grew closer as the years went by.

Even still, our growing bond didn't stop her from trying to tear me down mentally and emotionally. For Christmas, my cousins' gift boxes would overwhelm the bottom of the Christmas tree, while mine would be far fewer. When it was time to take family pictures with color-coordinated outfits, I held the bags and watched the children that were waiting on their turn. There was one professional picture where I was included, but since I was a last-minute addition, I stuck out like a sore thumb. My undone hair and all-black outfit completely clashed amongst the festive reds and fresh hairdos of her daughters. She was giving me insight into what she thought I was worth and making sure that I knew my place—the outcast; the motherless child; the one that everybody tolerated but no one really wanted around.

Deception and Depression

My aunt would set traps for me often to make me seem like a liar and deceiver. One family phone call might go well and on the next, I could be in a three-way ambush based on some random lie with no merit, bullied into submission with nothing short of brute force (even if it was just verbal and emotional). It got to the point that I began to have mini panic attacks when I heard that she was coming over to the house. I had to prepare my mind and think of every possible option of attack that she may have and try to be prepared for it. What did she have up her sleeve today? Had she called my grandmother ahead of time and fabricated some story about me? Did she sense that I was comfortable and wanted to play games with my mind? Or worse, was she just having a bad day and needed to take her anger out on somebody? I had seen my aunt angry, and she could be quite vicious when she felt disrespected. Anything could become a weapon and there would be no stopping her assault until her anger was fulfilled or she got tired. I was absolutely terrified of her as a child. She was a master of emotional manipulation and a violent woman whose strength could do serious damage when she was upset. I remember there being one instance where she threw my 13-year-old body clear across a room, sending me crashing into a metal closet door and breaking it off its hinges. What did I do, you ask? I hung up the phone on her just a few seconds too early, and she thought that I had intentionally hung up on her. The conversation itself was normal, all she was doing was calling to ask me to unlock the door so that she and her boyfriend could come in. Once the door was opened, I went flying, only hearing the reasoning for my abuse as I soared in midair on my way to the closet. I crashed into the door with literally no clue what hit me. She told me that I better never hang up on her again. I slunk off to my room to cry with both heart and body wounded. Why did she hate me so much? I still don't have the answer to this day.

A part of me gives her grace, because maybe she, too, was trying to care for me from an emotional storage that was depleted to a point. But the other part of me knows that there were many things that she did to me out of pure spite and malice, just because. She even spread lies about me around our neighborhood once I left. I'd hear about them from time to time and be both parts disappointed and unsurprised. She still does this even though I have no contact with her at all. She told my cousins—my sisters—that I was a traitor to the family and that anyone who had a relationship with me would be "banned." She did everything that she could to isolate me and make me feel alone in the world and tossed aside.

It's one of the most painful feelings in the world to be despised by someone that you love. My aunt was the last youthful link to my father that I had, and she wanted nothing to do with me. I think a part of me was desperately looking to her to be somewhat of a mother figure to me since she was closer in age to my mother than my grandmother. But my aunt denied me that bond time and time again, and still denies it, only feigning interest in me when she wants to rope me into something that she can hold against me later.

Who Am I?

As I matured into my adolescent years, I found myself reaching a breaking point. I couldn't hold the anxiety and depression and feelings of hopelessness in anymore. I was deteriorating mentally, emotionally, and spiritually. My house was full of people that I didn't believe loved me (even if it was a miscommunication), I was bullied relentlessly at school for being gangly, bigfooted, and four-eyed; and I had absolutely no friends. My grandmother needed me to help in and around the house, so I wasn't allowed to fraternize with the neighborhood kids or even go out to play. I only ever really saw the four walls of the house that I lived in and school. So, I watched, year after year, as all my classmates grew closer and made dates to meet at the mall and go to the movies. I watched enemies become best friends and best friends become family. I watched through the window as I saw groups of kids my age meet up with their friends and have long conversations just sitting on the curbside and laughing until dark. I wondered what they were talking about. I wondered what it felt like to have someone want so much to spend time with me that they would bear the mosquitos and the chill of the night just to hear the sound of my laugh. What did it feel like to be so loved and valued? What did it feel like to have friends like that? What did it feel like to be missed and accepted? Before long, the pit of depression in my stomach felt as heavy as a ball of steel, painfully applying pressure to everything that was inside of me. Every day it grew bigger and denser, threatening to drag what little life I had left in me out of me. I hated my life. I hated feeling trapped behind the locked doors of a house of people that didn't understand me and refused to nurture me. I hated the abuse that was compounding my PTSD and anxiety within me. I wanted to feel loved. I wanted to feel free. I wanted to feel like more than just a prisoner of my own mind and trauma and discontentment. I wanted to feel happy again, but I feared that I never would. And oh, how deep the sorrow goes when one feels like pain will never end. I wanted to end the pain. I wanted to end the grief. I wanted to end the sorrow, the anger, the bitterness, the brokenness, and all that came with it. I wanted to end it all.

I wanted to end my life altogether.

> *There is no sense in my cries and resent my eyes*
> *for shedding these two-bit tears!*
> *Reminding me always that no matter what I do,*
> *I'll give in to my stupid fears.*
>
> *Excerpt from "Makes No Sense"–written at age 15*

> *I've steadied my strut, but all seems vain.*
> *What used to drown in pain has been slain*
> *and now remains...emotionless.*
> *Only emotion is a notion, This devotion to destiny*
> *Getting the best of me before I shut down the rest of me.*
>
> *"Who Am I?"–written at age 16*

> *Look deep into the headquarters of my face*
> *and you still can't see*
> *how I wish I could replace*
> *my past or face last breath*
> *regretting not provoking my death.*
> *Excerpt from "Behind these Green Eyes"*
> *–written at age 15*

I knew that if something drastic didn't happen soon, I was going to die by my own hand. I just couldn't take it anymore. I even contemplated places to do it; somewhere in the open so that people could find me and see the manifestation of all the hurt that I felt. The only outlet that I had was writing, so I wrote feverishly about my intentions, penning multiple suicide notes through poetry. I was carrying burdens that no one knew the weight of, and I doubted that anyone, from strangers to school administrators, could even hold them long enough for me to take a breath unbridled. However, there was something in me that would not allow me to complete my suicide attempts. Every time I would get close to downing the pills, something would stir inside of me and make me put them down. I would see the knives and see my veins, but there would be something in my heart urging me to take a breath and take a moment to think. There had to be something more to life than what I was experiencing, and if there was, I wanted to see it. I just knew that there was more beauty to the world than the pain that I was experiencing and if I could just get out there, I could feel it for myself. That's when I decided to disrupt the cycle that I had found myself in. I was going to make my own rules and my own decisions, because at least if I fell on my path, then only I would be to blame for my pain and no one else. I was so tired of others causing me grief, so I decided to start making some bad choices and causing my own. I started lashing out, at my family first and then to any person of authority. I became self-serving and arrogant and incredibly disobedient. I started morphing into a young anarchist and began hanging around with the crowd that most resembled how I felt at the time–outcast. We created a family of misfits and only looked out for one another. If I didn't have the money to buy food at the mall, my food was covered. If I were having a horrible day emotionally, we would skip school and go to Taco Bell to talk or walk up and down the main street leading to our school. They became my therapists, defenders, and my family. They accepted me when nobody else would and didn't make me feel stupid or tainted or unlovable. I was finally a part of a group that saw me as an asset and not a liability.

The problem, though, was that I could only see my friends during school hours (since I was not allowed to see friends after school or on the weekends). I couldn't even talk on the phone to friends and barely talked to any other family either. I felt pulled away from the only people that made me feel good about myself and that stirred my resentment and depression more. So, I made up in my mind what I had to do to preserve my sanity and my life, and I took my grandmother's advice.

I was going to run away from home.

Chapter 3: Longing to Belong

I was only fourteen years old the first time that I ran away from my grandmother's house. I told her that I was going to the corner store (one of the few places that I was allowed to go from time to time) and instead of coming straight home. I just stayed outside. I stayed out for hours, fully inhaling my newfound liberation like the aroma of a new car, breathing in so deeply that even the air tasted different as it hit the back of my throat. I began to feel like I was fully exhaling for the very first time. This was uncharted territory. I had no plan of where to go, so I strolled through the streets of my neighborhood. Taking my time, walking slowly, enjoying the scenery. It was dangerous but felt divine. Of course, my grandmother had called the cops, and I was taken back home shortly thereafter, but I was already hooked. I was intoxicated with the scent of freedom and had to satisfy my lust for it. I walked the streets of my neighborhood with new freedom, feeling like I was finally in control of my fate. A police car met me soon after, and I was hauled back home.

> " *I felt like a hopeless castaway that no one cared for. I lived in a way that didn't regard death or life.*

I would run away off and on for the next two years. I had found a friend at my school whose house was a little more lenient than mine, and I would frequently spend the night at her house. I didn't ask for permission, and I didn't call my grandmother to let her know where I was. I just left when I pleased and stayed out as long as I wanted to. Eventually, my friend posed that I just come to live with her family. Her parents were much more relaxed than my grandmother and confirmed the invitation. I went back to my grandmother's house, grabbed some bags of clothes, and told her that I was leaving. No doubt this hurt her heart, but I was too high off my own sense of authoritative independence, and I had to do what I thought was best for me. I was about 15 or 16 years old at this time.

Looking back, my decision and my courage to do this was likely supported by my being under the influence. By age 14 or 15 that new sense of "freedom" had also extended to sex, drugs, and alcohol. I was 14 years old when I gave my virginity away to a junior at my school who broke my heart and told the school that I was loose. I started smoking marijuana around the same time. Age 15 brought the introduction of alcohol and daily cigarette use, and by age 17, I had graduated to ecstasy. I was so drugged out at such a young age that I'm surprised that there weren't lasting mental effects. I would pop single stacks, double stacks, and triple stacks of ecstasy recreationally, meaning there was no party or occasion other than me wanting to be high. I struggled so heavily with the pain of feeling detached from my brothers, the grief of losing both of my parents, the anger that stemmed from my relationship with my grandmother, and the resentment that I had towards my aunt. I felt like a hopeless castaway that no one cared for. I lived in a way that didn't regard death or life. I was completely lost and had no clue who I was. This is a void so deep that it can only be described by those who know its depth. The haunting pain of my broken life was consuming me from the inside, and I did anything that I could to try and silence it.

Longing to Belong

Who am I,
but a person who is stuck in the path of a wall?
Who am I,
besides an expressive mind, resisting protocol?
Never once being small, yet I feel I stand tall,
Which seems improbable, and is deemed impossible as
I stare,
unafraid, at my biggest invisible obstacle.
I feel ready, but ready for what?

Excerpt from "Who Am I?" – Age 16

I had left the nest but didn't know how to fly.

I left the imperfect security of my family home because I longed for a certain kind of love. A love that would shape me and answer all the questions that I had about myself and my worth. A love that would make me feel good. A love that my misguided heart would confuse with sex and sexual freedom while trading healthy physical affection for shallow sexual intimacy. I just wanted a love that I could feel, and a place where I could feel it. But I had no clue of what such "freedom" would cost me.

The Wounds of the Wolves

As I was struggling to find my way amid all that I had lost, I found myself clinging desperately to any shred of affection or attention that I could find. I wanted to belong. I desired to feel wanted passionately and not tolerated passively. I began to gravitate towards sex as a means of feeling some level of comfort. Molestation had already introduced me to a need to feel sexually stimulated, and the grief of losing so much of my family (either by death or separation) widened the chasm in my heart that desperately needed to feel one with something.

It was that ignorant openness that led me to lose my virginity at the tender age of 14. I characterize "losing my virginity" as my first sexual experience as a willing and knowledgeable participant. I gave something so precious to a boy that was three years older than me, all because he was the first male to show me some attention. He told me that he loved me, and that, "I wasn't like other girls my age." He said all the false affirmations that young eager eyes can't discern. I was an easy target with the makeup of a common casualty. A fatherless young runaway, with limited family ties and the mindset of a grown woman—I felt like I could do anything that I wanted to do without repercussion. Once he found out that I was a virgin, he made me the prime object of his affection until he got what he wanted. He saw the wounded desperation in my eyes and told me everything that he could to build a fantasy on my broken emotional foundation.

> " *Children only know what they're taught, and I was never taught to guard myself against men.*

I wanted to hear that I had found someone to protect me from all of life's trials and inconsistencies. I wanted to hear that I'd found someone who fully supported me and dared to stay long-term. I wanted to hear that someone could love me in a way that shook the very foundations of the world that I thought that I knew. A love that shook my world even harder than the trauma did. A love that healed all my broken pieces and held them gingerly as the fragile artifacts that they were. This guy told me that he was all of that, and I—eager to find something of my own though intoxicated by the scent of seduction—believed him. It was a long-term ploy of deception with an intent to steal the most precious thing that a young girl has. And in the end, though he cheated, he had claimed his prize. Once that happened, everything changed. I found out that while it seemed that he was wholly focused on me, he was in a relationship with another young girl whom he was expecting a child with. Upon confrontation, he told me that he was only there for the baby, but secretly there were more sinister levels to his plot to separate from his mark.

He started to become distant and elusive, leaving me to wonder if my frailties and shortcomings had pushed him away (insecurities that he would play on to gaslight me and justify his behavior). He avoided me like the plague and made it a point to slander my name throughout the school. He started to spread rumors about me, saying that I knew he had a pregnant girlfriend, and I was just an easy lay. Mind you, this was my freshman year, and he was a junior. He labeled me as a homewrecker that was trying to break up his relationship with his girlfriend. And what's worse, everybody believed him and shunned me for it. People didn't know who I was or what I had been through, and they didn't take the time to ask. They didn't know the bittersweet lies that he had been whispering into my naïve ears on all those nights that I had run away to be with him. They didn't know the piecrust-promises that he had made to me about our future and our love story, and they didn't care. All they knew was that I was a freshman, and allegedly, I was "fast." From that point on, I didn't know who I could trust, and who was just trying to get a slice of the pie that they were told was hot and free.

When my grandmother found out (I was still running in and out of her house at the time), she also attributed my experience to my being "fast" and said that I should have known better. She said that I should have "seen it coming" but, how could I? Children only know what they're taught, and I was never taught to guard myself against men. I was never taught the dangers of being lured away and deceived by the siren song of the pied piper. I was never taught how to vet lust from love. I was just expected to know. And we young girls, we don't know. That's the most dangerous part of the problem. Some things aren't intuitive and must be taught and taught well. I was ill-equipped and unprotected, live bait for any cunning predator (and he wasn't even really that cunning).

Sadly, what I hadn't yet realized was that the small wolf that had deceived me in the beginning was only a part of a larger pack. A pack of wolves that hunted specifically for young, wounded girls in a desire to devour them whole. And I, in my naivety, was like little Red Riding Hood—all dressed up to embark on a dangerous journey without the wisdom needed to survive the woods. It was this behavior that made me an easy target for larger wolves to come.

During that same year (my freshman year), I was tricked and sexually assaulted by a classmate under the threat of violence. He led me to believe that we were going to a mutual friend's house to smoke some weed (one of my newer vices at the time). As we walked down a hill, through a short, wooded area, he jokingly remarked about me performing oral sex on him. Immediately shocked and offended, I turned around and tried to walk back up the hill only for my path to be blocked. It was then that I noticed that my classmate's demeanor had changed. His body was tense, his eyes pierced, and his fists balled up at his side. He repeated his initial remark, but as a command, adding expletives. Tears began to flood my eyes as I clutched my red cloak and realized that I had certainly taken a wrong turn in the woods somewhere. I released all the air from my lungs as my chest heaved inward. His words had already knocked the breath out of me. My legs felt heavy, and my mind began to race. What's going to happen here? Will I survive this? What will I have to do to survive this? The way I saw it, there were only two possible outcomes; I could either: (1) remain calm and do what he demanded or (2) fight while screaming and risk being brutalized to an unknown end.

Luckily, and unluckily, I didn't have to make that choice. The guy, apparently nervous at the sight of my panic, suddenly begged me not to scream. I stepped back quickly and tried to retreat, but clumsily tripped on a tree root, and landed on my back. My abuser saw my posture as an opportunity, told me that I was beautiful, sat on my chest and took "matters" into his own hands. As I turned my head and closed my eyes, various emotions rose from the pit of my stomach: disgust, terror, resilience, and horror. But through it all, my mind could only muster one motivating phrase...*get through this moment alive*. With a blank stare, I gazed off numbly at the leaves of the trees and roots on the ground. I focused on the sky, and the sound of the birds, and before I knew it, he was finished. With my hoody stained and my life forever changed, I let him help me up. He told me that I could never tell anyone what he did, because it would be his "third strike." And I didn't tell anyone, not for another decade. Why? It was a mixture of things. Embarrassment from falling for a very easy to spot trap. Guilt over choosing to be passive and not fight back. The sheer shock and sadness that I even had to experience that from a fellow student that I thought I at least knew enough about to trust on a walk. But the biggest thing that shut my mouth was my proclivity to bury and be done with it. I had already developed a habit of swallowing my feelings to get through my day, and though this abuse was much harder to swallow, I still got it down in the end. This person and I even had mutual friends on social media for years, but I could never bring myself to share openly what he had done to me.

Foolishly, I charged it to the game of life and kept trying to move forward. I didn't realize that the acceptance of that assault ('acceptance' meaning my refusal to seek justice where due) was just the doorway to silently suffering from even deeper traps and more brutal assaults. I was sexually assaulted three more times before I graduated high school, all by different men and boys. Two situations were textbook sexual assault, and the other instance was outright rape. All of these scenarios ended just like the first, in that, I didn't tell anyone that they had happened until almost ten years later.

I naively entered the car of the man who would become my rapist because I thought that he was attractive. I was 15 at the time and thank God I'm alive to tell the story.

He was caramel-skinned, had hazel eyes, back-length dreadlocks, and his own car. He had to be about 23 or 24 at the time. He pulled up beside me as I was walking home from school and asked me if I wanted a ride. Seizing the opportunity to be in the company of an attractive man that poured attention where my insecurities hurt, I got into his car. This acceptance, in full disclosure, wasn't made under duress. I was just flattered that such an attractive, grown man was showing interest in me. It made me feel mature; Sexy; Independent; Alive. That's just me being honest. After all that I had already been through sexually, I was beginning to maneuver into a phase where I thought it necessary to be on the other side of my sexuality. The "other side" meant being the victor and not the victim. I wanted to be in control of sex for the first time in my life. I wanted to choose whether I engaged in sexual activity or not, and this action was one of my first missteps in that direction.

> " *I had gotten a little rougher around the edges and felt like I could handle anything that came my way.*

The man, we'll call him Rafael, said that he was going to the pet store down the street to pick up some fish and that he wanted me to help him pick one out. I took this as a cute gesture, like some impromptu date that I would see in a romantic comedy somewhere. My guards were completely down, and I felt that this was one of my first steps into taking back the reins of my sexual and romantic life. We chatted about different types of fish, and I began to ramble on about my favorite colors and some prospective fish names. The naivety of my 15-year-old mind still scares me to this day. Suddenly, I hear my fine friend Rafael laugh to himself and say, "Stupid," as if he was calling someone that by name. Stupid? Who is he calling stupid? I thought to myself. He answered my thought before I could ask audibly and told me that I was stupid. As he locked his car doors and leaned heavier on the gas, he began to tell me that I'm stupid for getting in the car with a strange man because I thought he was attractive. My stomach dropped and I turned my face to the window in utter panic and disbelief. "I could be taking you anywhere." He said with ambiguity. My chest heaves yet again. Looks like I made another wrong turn in the woods.

He continued to speed, and I began to wonder if this would be the last car ride that I'd ever take. After a few more miles, he slowed the car down and turned into the parking lot of the pet store. Now chuckling, he tries to reassure me that he was, "just kidding." I faked a laugh to mask my uneasiness. I wanted him to think that I knew what I was doing. We picked fish, Rafael cracked a couple of jokes, and then he took me home. I would learn later that it was a terrible mistake leading him there. Some months later—I think I was in my junior year of high school—I saw him again as I was walking to school in the pouring rain. A cable truck pulled up beside me and, you guessed it, offered me a ride to school. Frustrated by the rain and too upset to walk another two miles (I lived just outside of the line for bus pickup), I accepted the offer. At that point in my life, I had gotten a little rougher around the edges and felt like I could handle anything that came my way. That's what often happens when children become runaways that drink, smoke, and roam the streets.

Eve Before Fruit

I entered the van and thanked the driver, only to be met with a familiar face. We chit-chatted and in mid-conversation I called him by his name. He looked flustered and caught off guard, so I reminded him of our encounter months earlier (thinking it to be a power move on my part). He tensed up and I began to see something in him that I knew all too well. Sweat began to build on his forehead as he tried to play down his tangible discomfort. I couldn't figure out what made him immediately so uncomfortable but, looking back, it was likely because he was a repeat offender and wasn't used to seeing the same face twice. He drove me to school and gave me his cell phone number so that we could "keep in touch this time." I saved it into my phone, excited to have the number of a grown man with a job. Rafael and I began texting back and forth, and it was nice at first. However, after a couple of weeks his conversation with me started to send up some red flags. He would show me wads of cash and tell me that he would give it to me if I "earn it", and even suggested that I come to a party with him and some guy friends. I wanted no parts of that. I had become a little more street savvy since our last encounter, so I was able to peep game and decline all his offers. I lost interest in him after that, but he continued to reach out. I began to dread seeing his text messages and became shorter in my responses to him. Not too long after that, I decided not to talk to him anymore at all and requested that he leave me alone.

Suffice it to say, he did not like that.

He started texting me back aggressive messages asking me where I was so that he could come and see me. I told him to leave me alone and stop seeming so obsessed with me before I blocked his number. That comment may have been the one that set him off. I went about my normal schedule for the next few days, and I didn't hear another peep from Rafael.

It wasn't until I was leaving my house one morning, headed to school, that I saw a very familiar cable truck creeping slowly down my street. It was Rafael. He spotted me and hit the van's accelerator, speeding in my direction. I took off running. My neighborhood, at the time, was sectioned off into little blocks so ran down a one-way street to buy myself some more time. Unfortunately, he was smarter than that, and before I could make it to the next block, he cut me off and screamed at me to get into the van. Out of breath and feeling like a trapped fawn, my eyes darted left and right to see if there was anyone outside that could help me. The streets were empty, and everyone was inside so I panicked, and just got into the van. Rafael yelled profanities at me and complained about how much trouble I was for making him chase me.

All that I could do while I rode in his van was hold my breath and see how this encounter would end. I looked out the window the entire ride, trying to hold myself together and get my bearings as he drove in circles and in and out of my neighborhood. He took me to a back street and parked the van. Before I got a chance to ask him what we were doing parked behind a random house, he lunged toward me and yanked my legs onto the middle seat. He laid his full weight on my upper body as he quickly disrobed my lower half as if had done it a million times before. He whispers to me that he "had a dream" about this and prompted me to kiss him and make comments about his anatomy. He kept telling me to look him and look him in his eyes. How dare he violate me and try to make me look him in the face! The hazel eyes that had first attracted me were now bloodshot red and manic—nowhere near the warm and inviting hue that they once bore.

I soon realized that this wouldn't be over quickly, so I employed the only defense that I knew how. I pushed my protests deep down into the pit of my stomach and I froze in place. I numbed myself to survive that moment. With my face turned to the windshield, I focused on the clouds slowly shifting in the blue sky of the morning. I watched them without blinking, glassy-eyed and stone-faced. I gave him nothing that I could control—no reaction on my face and no satisfactory noises. Eventually, he put my limp hands behind his neck where I let them clasp lazily for the duration of the assault. All that I knew how to do was comply to get by, and this situation was no different. Once he finished, he gave me a vulgar compliment about my body and drove me the rest of the way to school. That was the day that I decided to live my life as emotionally numb as I could. That was the year that I added pills to my usual concoction of alcohol, marijuana, and cigarettes.

These encounters all hardened me in a way that nothing else ever could. These were wounds that ran deeper and deeper the longer that I let them fester. And I sat on these wounds for many years in hopes that the pain and shame from them would disappear if I didn't look at them. But that's not how life works, is it? I was apprehensive to share my assaults with anyone because I felt guilty and embarrassed about my responsibility in every situation. I was the one who got in the cars with strange men. I was the one who thought I was grown enough to handle wild wood situations though I was only a child. I was the one, wounded or not, who fell for every trap that was laid out before me. How stupid did that make me? I felt that if I told people what I had experienced, that I would be the only one to blame, and I didn't have room for any added layers of shame. In a way, each wolf swallowed a little piece of me, and the only way that I knew how to live with those holes was to keep myself numb to the fact that they even existed.

Instead of asking for help, or addressing my trauma head-on, I just wrote poems. I poured poetry out of my broken heart to relieve the painful pressure that I felt. I wrote poetry to keep myself sane, if only for a moment. The pain of everything that I had experienced, coupled with my fear of ever telling anyone, was slowly eating me up inside. All of the years that I spent crying over the loss of my parents, all of the hurt that I felt from being robbed of my innocence again and again and feeling like I had no advocate that loved me enough to see that I was bleeding finally came to a head. Drugs and alcohol became my comfort and escape.

And I wanted to die all the more.

It's sad to say that I have thoughts today of throwing every ounce of my life away,
Slitting my wrists and watching my blood run down like rain,
Tears of my pain…
An aspiring hero slain.

–Excerpt from "Crossroads" (Age 17)

Pain within my soul,
Anger within my heart,
how, if so, can my life restart?
A troubled child in a
troubled world struggling over dramatics and how my heartstrings curl,
I'm ready to die,
…and so, indifferent,
would stand the world…

–Excerpt from "Untitled" (Age 17)

If I light myself
afire, set ablaze,
Will it feel like
burning hell?
If I drown my lungs
in a liquid maze,

Eve Before Fruit

Would it relate to
how my eyes swell with tears of packed years of deep
pain and hurt that I doubt
I deserve?
If I decide to give
my life away and do end up in hell, how could I shift
it?
Then again, with hell
on Earth, would it really feel that much different?

–Excerpt from "Untitled" (Age 17)

A Mosaic of Broken Pieces

I had lost myself before I ever figured out who I was. All that I had become now was a mosaic of broken pieces and shattered dreams. A bag of shards that began to cut others without warning. I had no limits. I would pop ecstasy and walk the streets at night with my friend, feeling untouchable. I became a toxic friend with loyalty only to the love that I was seeking and not the people that had actually supported me. I was broken and breaking everything around me, and I hated myself for it. I didn't really want to be this ruthless person with no future and no friends. Deep down, I wanted to be much more. I wanted to be someone that my cousins and my parents could be proud of. I wanted to defy the odds that stared me in my face and declared death and depression over me. I desired to be a part of something greater than myself. I wanted my life to have more meaning and to serve some greater purpose. So, after just barely graduating from high school, I joined the United States Marine Corps.

The military would be the thing that would make me feel worthy and honorable. It was my opportunity to become someone respectable and loveable. It was my opportunity to be somebody. The Marines are known for being the toughest branch, and I needed them to teach me how to be tough. Tougher than every disappointment that was eating me up inside. Tougher than every disappointment that was eating me up inside. Tougher than the bruise and scars on my soul. Tougher than the fragile girl that life was eating alive. I wanted to feel powerful and in control of my future, and the military did that for me, temporarily.

My time in the Marine Corps served as the formative years for my adult life. I drank heavily, made friends that I will love for a lifetime, and made some very bad decisions rooted in unresolved emotional issues. I was my rawest in the Corps, but I think we all were. My service members and I would open up about our darkest places over drinks and cigarettes, tightly knitting our lifetime bond with one another. One thing about the military, if you didn't have much family when you enlisted, you sure left with a lot of family when you retired. My enlisted years were beautifully unforgettable, from hearing the historic blare of morning revelry to the proud sense of belonging that came with earning the blood stripe on my dress blues slacks, but inside of my soul there was still something daunting stirring. Like a whirling of toxic mist, my brokenness began to seep back up into my actions, countenance, and ability to connect with other people. It seemed that all of my broken pieces had missed the memo to stay home while I was away.

And not only did my trauma follow me there, but new trauma found me there as well. I experienced two more sexual assaults while I was active duty, with one assault being characterized as date rape with the use of a spiked drink. Both instances were by fellow Marines, the guys that were supposed to be looking out for me as a sister service member.

The glass ceiling on sense of security was cracking yet again and all I could do was run for cover. Why did this keep happening to me? Was there something about me that attracted these predators?

How many wolves did I have to encounter before I got to the other side of these woods?

I hadn't really started my life over by leaving my home state and joining the military. I was still the same broken girl dressed up in camouflage, only now I was even more broken. I was tired of being taken advantage of and tired of feeling like a helpless victim. I wanted to turn the tides of every area of weakness that I had and make it a strength. Instead of being the sexual victim, I decided again to become the seductive vixen.

From Victim to Vixen

Once again, I played the heavy hand and ended up tilted. I started my conquests by dating a married man (though he was separated at the time). I only had a couple of boyfriends and one girlfriend before this point, so this relationship was a stretch of my character. I was a risk-taker now. A woman in charge of her own destiny. A woman on a mission. A seductive vixen secretly driven by the motivations of the unloved young girl inside of her. I was still desperately on the hunt for real love. I drew close to any potential prospect like a moth to a flame, regardless of how unhealthy he was for me, because I had vowed to taste the warmth of love's fire even if I got scorched. There was still a great gaping hole on the inside of me that longed for affirmation and security, and I would have done anything to fill it. So, I used the only currency I thought that I owned—my body. I would take back my body from all my abusers that had misused it, and I would use my body to find the love that I desired. This way, instead of seeing my sexual brokenness, sexual partners would only see my innate sexual prowess. I thought to myself, *"This will make me worthy in the eyes of others."* I reasoned that this path—finding worth in sexual appeal and gratification—would lead to someone that would find me "worthy" enough to wed. Because honestly, that was all that I ever wanted. To fill the holes inside of me and be good enough for someone's "forever."

I wanted to get married to start a family of my own that would erase the pain of all the family that I didn't have. I wanted a family so beautiful that I would never feel the depths of loneliness again. I pursued this goal by trading sex for what I thought was security and stability. By this time, around the age of eighteen or nineteen, I had made up in my mind that everything was for sale while I was on my way buying a future of happiness. I began to narrow down the characteristics of my sexual exploits, deciding that I would no longer date women seriously, because I wanted to marry a man and have my own family naturally. I did still continue to pursue women sexually though. I let any woman that I encountered know that I just wanted to have a good time and to fulfill the lusts that had been pulsing in me for a decade. I was uncontrollable. Constantly feeding the beast, in a way. I had lust for women (wrongfully objectifying them due to early dreams and an addiction to pornography) but I would also lust after some men that I deemed as fun and not real prospect. I prided myself on my body and what it was able to do to sexually satisfy others, and myself. Sex was all that I thought about. I walked into coffee shops and grocery stores with lust on my lips and sex in my hips, scanning the room to see if my next partner was there. I measured people by their body parts and my perception of whether or not they would be fun to "play" with. I think that it was so easy to view others through the context of sex because that's how I viewed myself at that point. My merit and worth were determined by how sexy I could be or how many people I could tempt. I thrust myself in the waters of dating like live bait, hoping that something promising would bite. Dressing provocatively, flirting constantly, desperately doing anything to keep someone's attention. I became even worse when I was around men that I thought would make good husbands. I would change everything about myself to fit into the mold of that man's ideal woman.

I would do my hair like he liked it. I would dress in the way that he preferred. I would cut off friends if he told me to. I would settle for behaviors that were abusive and unloving, just to remain in the vicinity of the person that I had my eyes on and, hopefully, hooks in. I sold myself at a discount for any level of adoration, no matter how fickle. I gave everything that I had in every relationship that I was in and, instead of allowing the broken pieces of my heart to heal in between suitors, I just blew off the pieces and gingerly placed the crumbs in the hands of the next man who couldn't mend it. I became the obsessive girlfriend who didn't have a life outside of her mate. I would try to hide my trauma and only showed the "good parts," the goofball, the intelligent, the sweet side and the naughty side. Even flaunting my bisexuality as an extra bonus to dating me. I tried to be the perfect woman for every man that I came across to somehow trick him into marrying me. I didn't care that I had to swallow every feeling and settle for bad relationships with broken men that didn't love me as much as they said they did. If I was desired intensely, even if just for a moment and only in bed, I was satisfied. There was something about that feeling of being wanted more than anything in the world, even if just for a fleeting moment. My body gave me access to that feeling and I took it in as daily doses of the world's most lethal and addictive drug. I became a sex addict, chasing the feeling of being the most desired person in the world for only minutes or hours at a time. That feeling gave me power in knowing that I could bring a man to his knees if I willed it. Unfortunately, though, when the adrenaline stopped pumping and the feeling of ecstasy was over, I still was not good enough for him to want to marry me. Every breakup or rejection plunged the knife of depression deeper into my heart and begged the question: "Will I ever be enough?"

---

*I live subconsciously on the surface so that I don't slip
inside.
The black hole of my memories and the pain I try to
hide.
I walk a daily tightrope, faking every twist,
my balancing form is all too perfect,
simply because I do not exist.
"Me" lives in the heart of my solitude,
a child broken with faucet eyes,
whose larynx has been so worn out that it has no more
audible cries.*

*All the while the Dancer spins and glides,
Hungry for the audience's praise and cries,
But when she falls to her fate, due to a slight mistake,
the cheers turn quickly to hisses of hate.*

*This shell of a dancer has on a mask
Of the world's greatest clown,
Her movements she's mastered,
But behind the plaster,
Her eyes burn and tear to look down.*

*When in happenstance, she does flip and trip,
Proving herself to be a sham,
She regretfully falls deeper into the abyss,
That no one can understand...*

"Tightrope Dancer"–Age 18

I was struggling with a secret depression that no one knew about. It manifested itself in anxiety, one-night stands, abuse of prescription pills, and functioning alcoholism. I could drink a gallon of Moscato on a Wednesday night and go to work the next morning feeling refreshed. I drank in the mornings as I made lunch. I drank heavily in social situations (usually hard liquor) and have

Eve Before Fruit

been blackout drunk more times than I'd like to admit. The problem that no one saw was that a drink wasn't just a drink for me. It was a chance to escape the harsh reality of my existence. Drinking brought up every sore spot and I, in turn, tried to drown every weakness and heartache in pools of vodka and tequila. While everyone else was having fun, I was wondering if they could see past the cracks in my mask. Wondering if they could see the rusted chinks in my armor. Wondering when someone would notice that I am not as "together" as I pretended to be. It felt that I was always two people; the fun one on the stage that knew how to play to the crowd and the deeply depressed one behind the scenes that was blinded by the lights.

Sitting alone, in my own home of discontent,
My heart feels hard,
My ego scarred,
My patience far from spent.

A hollow shell, I've gone to hell, and come back in the clear,
A new person, I thought,
But I guess all was lost,
Because I'm standing right back here.

Back in my pit of sadness,
With my emotions and regrets,
I thought I had it figured out,
My world was all in check, no stress,

And yet, I'm down here, once again,
In this downhearted abyss,
It seems this pain is a boomerang that never seems to miss…

I swear I'll escape this fog one day, someway,
I know I can,

Longing to Belong

But until then, my happiness must live dormant,
In a cage that cage that no one understands.

"Untitled" Written in Marine Combat Training
–Age 18

It came to a point where it was evident that I needed to seek out a therapist, so that's just what I did. It was a move that I was initially afraid to make because who wants to admit that there's something wrong inside of them? I realized that it was high time for me to talk to someone objective about my feelings. A professional that could help me sort through all the tangles in my heart and give me some guidance on how to live my life. I was diagnosed with depression and adult ADHD. I opted not to receive any medication for the depression, as I didn't want to become dependent on it, but I booked visits with my psychologist weekly. There I was able to pour out of my deepest and darkest memories in a place where I didn't feel judged or compelled to act perfectly. I could articulate my wounds how I wanted to, cry if I needed to, and scream if I needed to as all was permissible within the four corners of my doctor's office. Therapy helped me tremendously by showing me that I was putting far too much pressure on myself mentally and emotionally. I deserved, and needed, time to heal alone. My doctor made me feel validated when I told her what I had experienced in life instead making me feel like baggage or someone second-class. For the first time, I felt human again. I felt seen in a healthy context and I didn't have trade a pound of flesh for it. Therapy was transformational…but it still had its limitations. The loudness of my trauma had deafened, this is true, but the effects of it kept cycling back around with no remorse. My depression would wash over me in large waves with weighty undertows. One minute I would be fine and out with my friends, and the next minute I would be sinking inside the black hole of my inner turmoil, unable to pull myself out.

Seasonal depression was the worst, especially around the holidays. That was the time where you saw the big Marine Corps family disconnect. People that I spent 95% of my time with took leave to go spend the holidays with their families. They would ask me what my plans were (usually I'd be working) and regale me with their plans to be gone for weeks on end. They would tell me about their family traditions and what uncle was flying in from out of state. I would listen to their stories with a smile on my face but inwardly, I was crumbling. What family did I have to go home to? Every other member of my family was either deceased or estranged, and I had no one. These were also the times that the grief of not having my parents with me dug a little deeper. Even when friends would invite me into their family's home, I would always feel out of place. I would be extra careful not to dirty the linen, extra courteous and polite and helpful—I would be "extra" everything, because I wanted to make the imposition of my presence in their home less noticeable. For I knew in the back of my mind that even if I had the time of my life at another family's house, reality waited for me at the door. I was a vagrant traveling from home to home and friend to friend, wishing that I had a place of my own to call home. My relationships still weren't working out and every breakup seemed to be a validation of my fear that I would always be alone. I was angry and full of resentment and therapy only cooled the fire in my heart, but never truly extinguished it.

> *Every other member of my family was either deceased or estranged, and I had no one.*

I needed hope for future-me that wasn't bound by past-me. I needed love. Real love. Love that would see beyond my past and elevate me to something greater—someone worthy—someone beautiful. But who could give me such a love and was it even real? So many had claimed to love me, but their "love" was never anything more than words in a text or in the dark. It was always far too fickle to hold long term or far too slippery to stay when the ride got bumpy. Was there one that would say, "I love you" and stay?

Was there one that would say they loved me and truly mean it?

He says he loves me,
As he takes away my youth,
He says he loves me as he tells me to disguise the truth
with lies that he's concocted,
Not knowing it was wrong, not knowing how to stop,
What can a 7-year-old say to an adult about the way
that he touches her?
What can she say about the "game" that they play
with no clothes, all toes and much—shame?
(he says he loves me)

Fast forward to the age of sexual maturity,
Flower already taken by moral impurity,
Why hold back now?
She gave, some took, some tried to take,
Some groaned, some groped, some tried to rape,
(he says he loves me)

and that's all she wanted to hear.
Exhortations of her beauty seemed to cure the fear that
she was ugly,
Even if only for a moment
(he says he loves me)

Tears fall down her face as she wishes she could erase
her past or face her last breath regretting not provoking her
death
(he says he loves me)

Eve Before Fruit

Beaten, bruised, and scarred,
Yearning for a healer for her already charred heart
(He says He loves me)
she hears a still voice in the night,
As she weeps in sobbing hands, it whispers,
"It will be alright."
(He says He loves me.), but just how can this be?

There're so many holes inside her now, so many voids
and cracks and pain.
She gave herself to anyone who would take her,
she gave in hopes to gain!
She's all poured out now, a hollow shell,
except for all the shame!
(Then, He says He loves me)

She says, "I don't know how that could be."
For what parts of me are left to love? What could you
possibly see?
(Still, He says He's loved me)

"Before I was in my mother's womb.
Had she known the pain I'd suffer, her belly would
have been my tomb!"
(Yet, He says He loves me)

Burning tears sear down her face,
"If you knew the muck I'd walked through,
You wouldn't embrace such a disgrace"
(Still, He says He loves me)

"But who am I to love?
Far too broken from pain unspoken. could my help be
from above?"
(He says He loves. me)

So, one day, she comes to Him.
Tired of running, tired of crying, tired of trying to run
from Him,
"Look, He says He loves me!

Longing to Belong

So, it doesn't matter if you don't,
And even if I fail to love myself,
He'll even love me where I won't!

He loves the broken pieces,
For there is a Golden Mend!
And no matter the shatters of the heart,
He can put them together again!

He says He LOVES me!
And the 'He' is Jesus Christ!
He is God, He is the Son,
and it is HE who's saved my life,
Because HE said HE loves me!!

Unconditionally.

Unabashedly.

Wholly and completely.

And that's all I needed to hear.
"He says He loves me."

"He says He loves me."

Chapter 4: Hearing the Voice of God
🎵 ·ıl|ı·.·

There was only one thing that had stuck with me throughout all my years of heartache. One unexplainable experience that kept me from killing myself in my darkest hours of depression and apathy. It was a voice. A voice that spoke to me and whispered in my ear that He, "had a work for me to do." This voice would come into my mind at the most random moments and tell me hopeful things about my future. It would say, "Let's go!" on the days that I regretted my eyes opening and wanted to stay sunken in my bed staring aimlessly at the wall. It said, "One day, you're going to marry a minister." in response to my tear-filled inquiry of what was going to become of my life.

> ❝ *I reasoned that the voice was God, but I wasn't sure which one.*

I still remember that night. I was an incredibly intoxicated teenager, and depression had just begun to pierce its talons through my bleeding heart. Sobbing quietly, my face drenched with tears, I looked up at the stars (the expanse of which had always calmed me) and threw my question up to the heavens. "What will become of my life?" And there it was, that voice spoke to me again and told me that I would marry a man in church. I responded with a scoff in disbelief, shrugging that notion off as a fabrication of my own mind. I didn't even go to church. In fact, at that point, I wouldn't have even known what type of church to go to! Before my father passed away, he was Muslim. My mother raised my brothers and me as Jehovah's Witnesses. At my grandmother's house we would watch Bible movies from time to time, but we never really went over scripture or attended any local assembly. There were also some Wiccans on my father's side. I was plagued by curses of their actions as well. I heard footsteps in the night when everyone else was asleep and have been paralyzed by shadowy figures staring at me on the side of my bed). The evil supernatural is certainly real, make no bones about that. I have seen it and experienced it for myself, and I can attest that evil spirits do exist and will plague a bloodline until someone stronger comes in and crushes their head.

But the one thing that the voice that spoke to me kept repeating was that He, "had a work for me to do." As crazy as it sounds, I would respond back to the voice and tell It that I wasn't ready. I reasoned that the voice was God, but I wasn't sure which one. I never told anybody about this while it was happening because I reasoned that it would be one more thing that made me less desirable as a friend and romantic partner. Every movie that showed a person claiming to "talk to God" showed that same person as fundamentally crazy and desperately mentally ill. Was I losing it? I didn't think the voice up, and it certainly wasn't my subconscious speaking to me. This voice showed me who my husband would be at a time where he, and I, were pursuing same sex partners. I didn't even know that young man at the time. He was just a boy walking down a ramp at my high school. No, this voice was something greater than me. And I truly believe that without that voice telling me to put down the pills, get up another day, "don't" run out onto the gun range, and "don't park" on this bridge, I would not be alive to tell this story today. It was the whispers of hope that rang in that voice that gave me the courage to turn from death every time it tried to seduce me. It was that voice—the voice of Jesus Christ—that I would come to follow in my darkest hour and for the rest of my life.

Lord,
I ask you to ….
Help me to open my
mind and heart so that I can hear you and stray from
all the things that will
cause me to falter.
Allow me the strength
and direction to manifest your will for me.
Make my blood thick,
so that it repels the sour water that is jealous of its
substance.
Mold Me into My
Destiny…
Amen.
–Untitled (Age 17)

After misplacing this poem for many years, I found it with my other poems and was baffled. When did I write this? When did I pray this prayer to the "Unknown God"? I called Him "Lord" as if I knew Him and prayed as if I had done it a thousand times before. I asked to hear Him and speak to me He did.

At the age of 22, I was honorably discharged from the military. I headed back to Maryland on the hope that I would live happily ever after with a man that I grew up with. When that didn't work out, I was forced to face the crumbled pieces of my identity as I sat in the state that started it all. I was no longer an active duty Marine with shiny medals and iron chevrons. I was no longer an ecstasy-popping child living at her best friend's house. I was no longer the apple of the man's eye that I had, once again, laid all my future hope into. Who was I now that all of the masks and crutches were gone? I was someone that hated looking into the mirror for fear of her own face. I was untethered, yet again, and feeling lost in the woods that I had faked mastery over for so many years. I had no home to go back to and, even if I did, I didn't know the way.

Thankfully, by this time, I had rekindled ties with the aunt that stopped me after my mother's death and reassured me that she would always be there for me. She began inviting me home for the holidays and even purchased my plane ticket a few times while I was active duty. I grew closer and closer to her and my cousins and clung to them as my sense of normalcy and tie to my bloodline. They were my anchors upon my return home, and we are still close today. I was the closest with my male cousin LaMar. LaMar and I would talk about life and crack jokes. We would always go out to bars and clubs when I was home on active duty leave. We bonded over rap, alcohol, and cigarettes, and he introduced to me his friends as his cousin-sister. But when I finally moved back home for good, He was much different than the LaMar that I knew before. He had quit smoking, quit drinking, and quit clubbing. He told me that he was living his life for God now and suggested that I do the same.

He invited me to church on numerous occasions, but I had always turned him down. Church and I didn't have a good reputation. I had had plenty of friend's take me to their churches over the years and the same thing always ended up happening. As praise and worship was going on, I would feel a tug in my heart that pulled up all the muck and pain that I had buried deep inside. As much as I tried to hide, the years would flow out in tears and I would sob profusely. Those looking on could tell that my cry wasn't superficial, that it groaned from a place of pain far deeper than one church service could heal. A place far deeper than they knew even existed inside me. Afterwards, I would feel embarrassed as I tried to gather all the evidence of my trauma and stuff it back down into the vault that I kept it locked in. It never worked. People had already seen the weight that I was carrying and I, too nervous to unload my baggage in an unsafe place, would never let anyone try to help me. I eventually stopped accepting invitations to churches altogether. And this is exactly what I told my cousin. I said, "If I don't like your church, then it's going to affect our relationship, and I think we got a good thing going on." He then asked me something that I know was inspired by God Himself. He said, "But Fetima, don't you want more?" I froze in that moment, trying to maintain my face as my soul began to weep—bothered by the fact that its brokenness had once again been summoned. The "more" that he mentioned was all that I had ever wanted for my life. Something more than the trauma. Something more than the trauma. Something more than rage. Something . . . more.

My cousin's question had knocked on the door of my quivering heart and challenged it. "Fetima, don't you want more?" It was that question that led me to visit my cousin's church. I was at the end of my emotional rope and felt like this was a time to finally try something that I hadn't pursued before. I was finally going to let go of my grip on my pain and hand it over to the God that I had been running from. The God that spoke to me in my head (if my cousin's god be that God). The God that had kept me alive because He, "had a work for me to do." This would be the beginning of the end of my life as I knew it.

Old Body, New Birth

I chose to visit my cousin's church on a Friday night because I felt that it would be less intimidating for me. I was wrong. From the minute that I walked through the doors, I felt like every eye was on me. I was reeking of vodka from partying the night before—a last hoorah before I turned my life over. It was my good friend's birthday party, but that night meant something so much more to me, so I drank much more than I usually would. So much so, that the smell of the liquor that I had ingested the night before still clung to my pores the next day. I had a hangover in my head but determination in my heart. I can't even remember what the sermon was about, but I do remember how I felt there in the presence of God. It felt like 'home' to me. This is the church where I experienced the presence of the God that was speaking to me in my head. People spoke in a different language here. A heavenly language that they said only God could give you. The Bible called it the Holy Ghost. I saw a man being used by God to speak prophetically to the congregation. My cousin asked me if I was alright afterwards, because sometimes an experience like that can scare people away, but I was fine. That night stirred up a curiosity in me. Was this the operation of the God of the Bible? I came back to LaMar's church that Sunday and the Sunday after that. My curiosity had been peaked, and I wanted to see if there was something to this God and this "church thing." I knew how the presence of evil spirits felt, but I had never felt a spiritual presence like this before. This presence had substance and depth and felt comforting to me. I yearned to hear about this God.

One day, while the Bishop was preaching about the salvation experience, he lingered a little while on baptism. He spoke with passion, explaining that we are, by nature, sinful creatures. Not only of our own accord, but by birth, from the first day that we entered the earth. Sin had entered the world and corrupted the original perfection of God's creation. The only way to remove that sin is to confess and repent of our sins (now understanding the knowledge of our innate sinful nature and our expressed sinful deeds committed in the body), be baptized in the name of Jesus for the remission of those sins, and be filled with the Holy Ghost to have power over the powerful temptations of future sins. It was the repentance part that challenged me first. Repentance meant to admit to God that I was living my life in a sinful way, understanding that I was innately sinful as a human being, and to turn from the way that I was living. I thought to myself, "What do I have to repent for when I am the one who has been through so much at the hands of others!? When I have been the one that has been abused and raped and cast aside! When I am the one who lost my parents and never felt loved! Of course, I acted out. Who wouldn't?" I was perplexed. What could I owe anyone, especially God, when the world owed me so much because I had endured so much?

Well, the answer came quickly to those questions by way of God's conviction. My first mistake was believing that the world, and everyone in it, owed me something when I was already born with a debt to pay to God Himself. Not just because of what I'd done, but because of the nature of who I am, my love for sin and my will to rebel against the One that created me, deteriorating the very health of my soul. A nature that was innate in my members, keeping me enslaved to its wills and feelings and desires for my life. A nature that kept me separated from the God that loves me so dearly. I was naked in the garden yet again. Found guilty in the presence of all that God had created, standing bare in my sin before the One who only wanted to have a deeper relationship with me. I could barely speak or move in His presence. The voice that had always spoken to me of beautiful things and future hope now called me condemned. Because of this, I could not follow Him like I was, treading sin into the holy plan of God for my life like the muddiest shoes on a freshly white carpet. Instead, He offered me a choice: Repent and allow Him to clean me through the Blood of Jesus, granting me access to wonders and revelations untold, or stand in the filth of my sins and never let my feet touch the magnificent grounds of Heaven.

It was a hard pill to swallow initially but I eventually found this truth to be refreshing. This was beautiful because the heart of the Gospel is understanding that though I was born sinful and should be condemned by a holy and just God, Christ, through His sacrifice in my place, covered the effects of that nature under His blood thousands of years before I was ever conceived! God had spoken the truth of my existence (the bad news) but already had the hopeful remedy for my sins in place (the Good News). Just like God had spoken in Genesis—that the serpent would bite the woman's son on the heel (speaking of the crucifixion of Jesus)—He also spoke that this same Son would crush the serpent's head at Christ's resurrection, and finally when Jesus throws Satan into the lake of fire at the end of all of this. God knew the end of the story before the beginning had even occurred, and so too, did He know the beautiful victory of my ending before the pain of my beginning had even occurred. Though sin ruled in my members, God was offering me a way to be free. I had to repent for how I allowed the anger from my trauma to manifest in my life and in the way that I treated others. I had to repent for drowning my depression in vodka and wine, and not handing it over to the God whose stripes bore my healing. I had to repent for living my life like God didn't exist even though the voice that spoke to me in my head always reminded me that He did. I had to repent for living my life as an enemy of the God that died and rose again so that I could be called His friend.

Finally, God had turned my weeping face to His, and I had decided to look Him square in the eyes. He said He loved me, and that was all that I needed to hear. I wanted what God was offering me. I wanted to be made over. I wanted to be made new. I had always wondered and wished that it were possible to start life over again and now I was faced with the

> " *I would finally be able to breathe again after decades of feeling like I was holding my breath.*

opportunity. I wanted a life that wasn't bound or defined by my brokenness. I desired to be separated from all that I had done and all that was done to me. And what I wished, thank you Jesus, had already been written in a Holy Book that I had never read. That book was the Bible, and it told me that the keys to my freedom were crafted by every scar in Jesus's whiplashed back. It told me that my sin was borne on the back of a man that knew no sin and was washed by the blood and water that poured out of Him for me. The Bible said that, just like Christ, I must die to my flesh and be born again by the Spirit of God. Christ had died so that the new Fetima could live.

I would finally be able to breathe again after decades of feeling like I was holding my breath.

As I contemplated answering the call to the altar, I immediately became gripped in fear and anxiety. I didn't know anyone at that church except my cousin. What would people think of me if I stood up and stood out? Could they see the sins that I wanted to wash away in the water? Could they feel the depths of the mud that I had walked through? Did I finally have the courage to take my first steps in faith instead allowing my fear to swallow me whole and hinder my path?

It was there, in that moment, that God spoke to me yet again. He said, "Seek me in the water." I get chills thinking about it even now. The water was a place that I would always go back to when I was feeling stressed or overwhelmed. No matter what state I was living in, I always found a lake or some like body of water to wash away my overflowing anxiety with the tide. The horizon of ocean water calmed me because it reminded me that the world was so much more expansive than whatever heartache that I was dealing with. The still water of a lake set the serene tone that I needed to calm the raging seas of my emotion before I was caught up in the undertow. And in that church, on that Sunday morning, the water was calling me yet again. The water was telling me that healing and peace was upon it, not because of the water's makeup itself, but because of the Blood of Jesus that it represented. It could have been any water that I found myself beside that day. But God told me to seek Him in that water, and I said, "Thy face Lord will I seek."

Baptism

I had heard so much about what the freedom of baptism could do for someone and I was ready to seek that freedom for myself. I was so convinced about the cleansing power of the Blood of Jesus that I believed that my tattoos would be left behind in the water. I had been looking for a way to be new and this baptism into new life was just the thing that I had been waiting for, nay searching for, all my life. So, I leaned over to my cousin and told him that I wanted to get baptized. I had made every excuse imaginable up until that point (i.e., my hair will be ruined, my makeup will be ruined, my clothes will get drenched, etc.), but God had made sure to choose the day that I was running late for church—with undone hair and no makeup—to reintroduce His original proposition. "Seek Me in the water." God's words echoed through my head as I began to realize that the events of my morning were not just coincidence, but divine providence. My cousin agreed to walk with me to the altar so that I could receive prayer and make the ministers aware of my decision to be baptized. Every step toward the front of the church felt foreign, like I was learning to walk for the first time. My feet felt shaky and unsure, but my soul was determined. It had carried many wounds for many years and drowned in many tears, and it longed for a rest from its burdens. I was on my way to "trouble the water" and feed it all that ate me up inside. I was going to be cleansed of my sins and past transgressions. Cleansed of my old life and old ways. Cleansed of my ideas of who I could and could never be. I was on my way to the Heart Fixer, and I had many broken pieces to mend.

I could barely think straight as I disrobed and changed into my all-white baptismal gown. I thought to myself, "This must be the first illustration of what I'm about to experience—exchanging my colored clothes for a white robe." As I was led to the pool, the entire church congregation stood on their feet in solidarity of my sacrifice to God. They were singing praises aloud, but I could barely comprehend their voices, because in my mind I was already under the water. I was asked the question, "Do you believe in the death, burial, and resurrection of our Lord and Savior Jesus Christ?" I replied in the affirmative.

"Upon the confession of your faith, we now indeed baptize you in the name of Jesus Christ for the remission of your sins, and you shall receive the gift of the Holy Ghost. We baptize you now, In Jesus's Name."

I was dunked backwards into the water until the waves of the pools came up on both sides and fully submerged my body underwater. I arose from the water gasping as a newborn babe, with a smile beaming from ear to ear. I had finally done it! I had finally taken the first step of the rest of my life, and I could now move forward into my healing, unashamed!

I was 23 years old and the date was March 10, 2013. I will never forget that day. In fact, I celebrate it every year. That baptismal water took away the stains of twenty-three years of physical trauma and emotional agony leaving the slate of my life washed clean. I was new just like I had always wanted to be, but this experience was only the beginning.

Though I had attained a new lease on life, I still needed strength and supernatural power to help me overcome the old Fetima and walk fully in the new. Change takes work and it is not usually completed in one fell swoop. Lifelong habits can take years to break and this Christian walk required me to exchange everything that I thought I knew about myself or about the world for what the Bible says about it. Instead of believing that I would always feel alone and broken, I had to believe God when He said, "I will not leave you comfortless, I will come to you." I had felt cast aside and unseen, but God told me that He wouldn't leave me alone or without comfort. He promised to meet me wherever I was pouring out and nurture me to emotional, mental, and spiritual health just like a father would.

Instead of believing that my life was just a pointless muddle of tragedy after tragedy that had no end, I had to believe God when He said, "For I know the plans that I have for you. thoughts of peace and not of evil, to give you an expected end." I had begun to feel that my life could never be better than the brokenness that it was, but God challenged me to trust that He had a plan for me. Instead of believing that I was worthless and unwanted, God wanted me to know, with assurance, that even the hairs on my head are numbered and He knows them all.

It's a beautiful thing to know that you were intricately formed by God inside of your mother's womb and not just a fortunate (or unfortunate) chemical accident in the heat of passion. To know that you were born with purpose in the mind of the God that spoke the world into existence with the breath of His mouth. It's an unexplainable feeling to go from worthless to worthy in the sight of a holy god. All I needed now was the power to war against my natural tendencies and maintain the purity that baptism granted me. I needed to be filled with the Holy Ghost.

The Holy Ghost

The Bible says that after you receive the Holy Ghost, you now have supernatural power. Power to war against the enemy of your soul and all his minions. Power to win over the harmful vices and coping mechanisms that crippled you more than helped you. Power to face every internal obstacle that you were too afraid to even look at in the mirror. Rest assured, there are some things in our lives that only the Holy Ghost can heal.

The Holy Ghost is a part of God that He allows you to borrow while you live here on earth. It's a piece of God that He allows to dwell within you to guide you in His ways and not your own. It's the Comforter that He said would come to you. The experience of receiving the Holy Ghost is something that cannot be denied or explained by science or medicine. It feels like being internally warmed by a roaring fire that springs up from your belly and pours out from your mouth in a heavenly language that your tongue has never uttered before. This is a language of angels that only God can interpret fully. It's a language that flows from the corners of your heart and spills out in sounds and tones that you could never even think to say. This is the Spirit of God speaking through you, to Himself, on your behalf. God literally gives you a piece of Himself to intercede for you when you don't know the words to pray. How amazing is that?

I remember when I first received the Spirit of the eternal God into my mortal body. Our Bishop had preached a few days prior about the power of the Holy Ghost. He said that the Holy Ghost not only gave you power to remain pure and strength in a time of need, but He also will protect you against the possession of evil spirits. I had experienced bullying from evil spirits all my life, from tangible presences to horrific and violent dreams, so I already knew that the demonic realm was real and active. I just didn't know why I experienced demonic attacks so frequently (though I'm learning that answer more and more now). So later, while I was in my room, I called God out on His word. I said, "They told me that the Holy Ghost could give me power and strength to fight against demonic forces. If it's real, I want it." I paused and closed by eyes for a moment, meditating on what I had just asked of my Savior. Then, suddenly, I became overcome with a sensation that I had never known before. I felt hot all over, but I was trembling, and I fell to the floor and laid there. Something was bubbling up from my depths inside me, and my mouth filled with the slurred speech of a baby just learning how to form words. And then it happened! I let the Spirit of God take control of my tongue, and out of my mouth flowed the language of angels! I had been filled with the Holy Ghost!

And who did I call first? My cousin LaMar. I could barely speak earthly words in the middle of the heavenly syllables. LaMar burst into tears on the phone, overwhelmed with joy at the progress that God was making in my life. On that night, March 17, 2013, I was sealed until the day of redemption by the Spirit of the Lord.

After receiving the Holy Ghost, I started to pray more, pray longer, and pray more earnestly. If this was how God was going to change my life, then I wanted to finally pour out everything from my fragile heart that I had been holding back from him. All my pains, all my hopes and aspirations. All my fears and reservations. I wanted to know if God was as real as the Bible said that He was. Would He really come to me in the middle of the night when I am under demonic attack and intimidation and war on my behalf—sheltering me under His shadow as every arrow flew? Would He really bottle every tear that I cried, even the ones that got trapped in my throat that I couldn't utter? Could He really turn the ashes of my past into beauty and give me the oil of joy for my mourning?

The process of learning the answers to these questions was not what I had initially expected. The healing of my heart and the renewing of mind was not an instantaneous thing that happened when I wanted it to. It was going to take faith, and work would have to be added to my faith for me to lay hold to all the promises that God had for me. It would take the Blood of Jesus, sweat and many tears to make my stony heart a heart of flesh, but God had already spoken that He was able. Now it was time for me to prove that I was willing.

Chapter 5: Learning to Walk in the New

With this newfound strength and purpose, I sought God more earnestly. I wanted to know who God saw when he crafted me in Patricia Ann's belly. What prophetic words did He speak over me? What gifts did he whisper into the strands of my DNA?

What was the strength of my voice before all of life's trauma had silenced it?

What was I purposed to accomplish even before corruption crossed my path?

Who was the Fetima that God had in mind's eye when He breathed my soul into existence?

> **"** *I asked God to hit the 'reset' button on my life to start my entire existence on this earth anew.*

I decided to embark on a journey with Christ to find out. I prayed, and I asked God to hit the 'reset' button on my life to start my entire existence on this earth anew. I wanted to become the woman that I would have been had I never been molested, or raped, or addicted to drugs or sex or alcohol or attention. I wanted to become the woman that I could have been before depression took my mind and suicide haunted my thoughts. I needed God to reach back into the years of my life and heal me in every area that I was broken. I needed Him to go back in time and reset the course of my life. If I was truly going to be a new creature, I wanted to become the creature that God had created in me from the beginning. Like Eve, before she had tasted the forbidden fruit; her potential unbridled, her innocence intact, and her purpose coursing through even the very marrow of her bones, unrelenting. I needed God Almighty to make me new and to change my name, and I refused to leave Him alone until He blessed me.

I knew that my journey of healing would take some work, but I had faith that God would help me wade through the muddy waters of the bog that filled my heart and clean me from any algae that clung to me. I had been made into a new creature spiritually, but I needed God's help to show me how to act like a new creature, love like a new creature. I needed God to guide my eyes to the mirror so that I could see that I was a new creature. That I wasn't defined by my past or wounds or any hateful limitations that others had placed on me. I wasn't who my fear and anxiety said that I was—I was a child of God, walking in the power and authority of the One that had created me. I wasn't the broken and wounded girl that life chewed up and spit out—I was the one that God called His own as He was knitting me in my mother's womb. His plan for me had never faltered, but there were waters that I needed to wade through to be able to get to where I needed to be in God.

Healing Hurts

Healing can be challenging. In fact, if healing doesn't make you a little uncomfortable, how will you know you've cleaned the wound out to the bottom? Alcohol stings when you're sanitizing an open wound and even braces hurt while you endure the slow process of straightening your teeth. Healing with God is just the same. The gospel of Christ is not just about the "fluffy stuff" (i.e., being kind and being generous), it challenges you to love your enemies and to pray for the people that use you and persecute you. It challenges you to give without expecting to receive anything in return. It challenges you to forgive repeatedly as God forgives you, lest your repentance be found on deaf ears.

> *It is God when I can forgive someone who has done the 'unforgivable.'*

Soon after I had received forgiveness for my sins, God reminded me of the sins of others that I had left unforgiven. In a very gentle and loving way, He nudged me to offer to others the same thing that He had showered upon me—grace. Namely, He wanted me to release the burdensome offense of the first person that had harmed me—the man that first molested me as a young child.

Make no mistake, God is genuinely concerned about the corrupted innocence (sexual or otherwise) of children. Childhood is often the place where the devil likes to corrupt a life or an entire bloodline. Additionally, if you corrupt children at a young enough age, you can disrupt the course of their identity for the rest of their lives. That instance becomes the moment where the eyes of the child opens to the dangers and failures and evils of the world around them. That is the true corruption of that child's innocence.

I had grown to hate and resent the person that took mine.

Hatred eats away at the very fabric of the fleshy heart, devouring it whole if left unhealed for long enough. But God, being a specialist in all things that hurt the heart, prompted me to forgive the man that had done the unforgivable to me. It was a hard task to hear, but I realized that, through this action, God was giving me (little by little) what I had prayed for. The remedy for hatred that hurts the heart is true compassionate forgiveness. It's the love that God sheds for us given to those in our lives that need it the most. It's the kind of love that brings you to your knees and lifts your tearful eyes toward Heaven. That's what God had given me… and He wanted me to dish it out.

Forgiving the Unforgivable

True forgiveness is birthed out of an earnest compassion that only God can release inside of you. It breaks the chains off your heart, allowing you to be seated in a place where God can pour out abundant blessings into open hands with wrists not bound by bitterness or resentment.

It is an absolute supernatural miracle when you can forgive your abuser.

God birthed this miracle in me. I was completely fine with never speaking to that particular family member again, but God challenged me to see him as a broken vessel that was also made in the image of God. Just like my trauma had affected me and caused me to hurt others and myself, his trauma had led him down the same path, with a different outcome. I was not more worthy of forgiveness than he was—not in the eyes of God Almighty.

> *" My abuser cried on the phone with me, and I could literally feel the torment that was gripping his heart.*

So, after much prayer, I decided to reach out to him. I reminded him of what he did to me (because you can't clean a wound that you're too scared to lift the bandage off) and told him that in spite of how it affected me, I wanted him to know that I forgave him. As those words exited my mouth, I felt a pressure in my chest release. The knot that had been in my stomach unwound, and I was finally able to speak freely and really hear what my family member had to say. He wasn't a monster with red eyes and gnashing teeth and claws for hands. He was a person that had been abused himself, and he had lived buried under the shame of what he had done to me since the day that it was exposed. My abuser cried on the phone with me, and I could literally feel the torment that was gripping his heart. He told me that he had no reason or excuse for what he did, and he wished that he were dead because of it. I could tell that he was serious.

It was in that moment that God took the miracle of forgiveness and pressed it in a bit further. The Spirit of God egged on by God's love for even my abuser, rose in me and began to tell him about the freedom and power of forgiveness through Jesus Christ. I told him that no matter what he had done, to me or to others, God will still hear him and forgive him if he repents. I ministered to him about the beauty of baptism and what it symbolized. I told him about how receiving the Holy Spirit could give him power over any perversion and lustful curiosities that had power over him. It was because God allowed me to see my abuser as a soul, and a human being, that I was able to share with him the freedom that I had found in Christ. I let him know, with no hesitation or bitterness in my heart, that if God could save me from my sins, and myself, then He could do the exact same for him.

Resentment and anger wouldn't have allowed me to utter any of those words to my family member. Unforgiveness would have me shut my mouth and sit on the very thing that would save his soul and create generational change in his life and our bloodline. But human compassion, fortified by Jesus Christ Himself, allowed me to give my abuser and myself the greatest gift that I ever could, forgiveness.

Resentment and anger can act as a chokehold or heavy yoke around your neck, keeping you imprisoned by the memories of your trauma. Memories that only display your abuser as the monster that goes 'bump' in the night, or the thief that swindles you into allowing them to take your most valuable possessions. But what God helped me realize was that unforgiveness was truly my enemy. That was the thing that would have hindered me to my grave. Not the pain, but the poison of hatred and unforgiveness.

It is good when I can forgive someone who has done a light thing to me. It is GOD when I can forgive someone who has done the "unforgivable."

Forgiving without Apology

The next person that God laid on my heart to forgive was the aunt that had always tormented me. We went from executing one hard act of supernatural grace and kindness to the next! But God assured me through His Word that He would never leave me or forsake me. He had asked me to execute another hard task, but His strength and His presence would be with me. What made this situation different, however, was that my aunt was still being terrible towards me and trying to turn people against me! I didn't see how I would be able to walk in strength and forgiveness in the face of someone who was unrepentant about being so cruel to me. But as is the case in many scenarios, many times, God will show us better than He can tell us.

After years of avoiding my aunt (for obvious reasons), I found myself in the same room as her, standing in proxy for another relative whose life she was trying to derail. My presence alone enraged my aunt enough to cuss me out and threaten my life in front of other family and onlookers alike. Though I was 25 years old at the time, my body still went into complete shock. It responded to the threats and public embarrassment just as it would have had I still been a young, helpless child with no way of escape. As I sat there being berated, my legs felt like lead being prodded by electric currents. My stomach became weak and my body began to tremble uncontrollably. I was having a full-on anxiety attack. I couldn't even lift my eyes from the floor as my ears rang with her insults. With clammy hands, I fiddled with my fingers, trying to muster up at least enough strength to keep the tears from falling down my face. I was in an unrelenting panic, but I didn't want to show the truth of how terrified I was inside. In a matter of minutes, the verbal assault was over, but the whirlwind of the all-too-familiar feelings of anxiety and paralyzing fear were left still lingering. On top of that, there was the added disappointment that I felt in myself for failing to self-advocate when the attack was happening. I let her punk me in public, yet again, and I was mad at myself for it. How could I have allowed her to make me feel like a child again after so many years?

It was a classic case of PTSD muscle memory. Though I was an adult, the events of that moment had taken me back to a place in my childhood where I remembered how volatile my aunt's emotions could get, and how violent and cruel she could be as a result. It's like the story of the little circus elephant anchored to the ground by a string and stick. When the elephant was a baby, all it took was that flimsy contraption to keep him stuck in one position. No matter how hard he fought, the tension of the string and the stick in the ground always won. It happened so many times that it became ingrained in the young elephant's memory. So much so that as the years went by and the elephant grew large enough to physically free himself from the lowly bonds of the string and the stick, all that flooded his mind were the memories of his childhood failure and futility. And so, the elephant, far large enough to rip the stick from the ground and tear the string to pieces, never even tries to escape. The elephant's memories, aside from his obvious strength, are what keep him immobile and tethered to the ground. And that is what I had to learn of myself. It wasn't the fact that I wasn't strong enough to fight back or to defend myself, it was that my mind and body remembered how helpless I used to be in situations like that one. Year after year, that terrified response was what my body had adopted to protect itself when I couldn't. It was ingrained in my members to fear her. And in that moment, of realizing the childhood muscle memory of my adult body, I decided that I needed to run to the best advocate that I knew…and that was God Himself. When I returned home from that encounter, tears streaming endlessly down my face, the first thing that I did was cry out to my Heavenly Father. I begged Him to stir up the power and the sound mind that He promised me in 2 Timothy 1:7. As I prayed, in tongues and in earthly words, God led me to read and pray according to the verses in Psalms 27. He whispered to my heart and said, "Seek my face."

Verse 1: THE LORD IS MY LIGHT AND MY SALVATION; WHOM SHALL I FEAR? THE LORD IS THE STRENGTH OF MY LIFE; OF WHOM SHALL I BE AFRAID?

If God is my strength and my refuge—the Creator of all who is larger and more powerful than any created thing. why should I fear any other person if He is with me?

Verse 5: FOR IN THE TIME OF TROUBLE HE SHALL HIDE ME IN HIS PAVILION: IN THE SECRET OF HIS TABERNACLE SHALL HE HIDE ME; HE SHALL SET ME UP UPON A ROCK.

When I am afraid and trouble is surrounding me, my God will hide me in a safe place and establish my feet in security.

Verses 7-8: HEAR, O LORD, WHEN I CRY WITH MY VOICE: HAVE MERCY ALSO UPON ME, AND ANSWER ME. WHEN THOU SAIDST, SEEK YE MY FACE; MY HEART SAID UNTO THEE, THY FACE, LORD, WILL I SEEK.

God, You are showing me that the only way to endure hard trials is to seek Your face, through tears and prayers, and listen to Your voice for instruction.

Learning to Walk in the New

Verses 11-14: Teach me thy way, O Lord, and lead me in a plain path, because of mine enemies. Deliver me not over unto the will of mine enemies: for false witnesses are risen up against me, and such as breathe out cruelty. I had fainted, unless I had believed to see the goodness of the Lord in the land of the living. Wait on the Lord: be of good courage, and he shall strengthen thine heart: wait, I say, on the Lord. (KJV)

It is difficult to be berated by a loved one or to be lied on by anyone, but please lead me in the way that I should go, so that I don't fall victim to any trap that is set before me.

Notice the connection between what God whispered to me and what had already been written in verse 8 of Psalms 27. The Lord was letting me know that there was a timely message for me in the scriptures that had been written so many years ago. I heard Him, through His Word, resounding the sentiments of my broken heart through a prayer that was written by David thousands of years before I was ever even a thought. God was reminding me that there is, "nothing new under the sun", and letting me know that even David had problems with people, but he also had the faith to believe that the hand of the Lord would lift him up. I prayed that very same prayer that day. Breathing verse 13 with a sigh of relief as the last tears fell from my face, I spoke, "I had fainted unless I believed to see the goodness of the Lord in the land of the living."

My aunt was another family member that I had hated for many years and resented for many more. I just never understood how someone who was supposed to be my family, someone who mourned for the same familial deaths that I did; someone who watched me grow up, could have such an unwarranted hatred for me. It hurt me because I truly did love her, and I still do (regardless of how harshly she treated me). Because the problem wasn't just how she treated me, it was the fact that I loved her and desperately wanted that love to be reciprocated that hurt so much.

I truly hated her until I learned the very important lesson of being able to see her for who she is. She is a woman who has also endured much heartache in her life. She is a woman who has understood deep, deep sorrow—and those emotions can wound you in ways that are irreparable without a Savior. I've learned the beauty of giving her grace (while still executing distance and wisdom). I've learned to pray for her needs as a person, and petition healing for her heart as a soul loved by the Almighty God. I've learned that we all have things that we're working on that affect how we view and interact with other people—whether our work has been fruitful or not.

Though this woman had hurt me more than anyone else and was the reason why I was paranoid about trusting people, if I expected to move forward in my life at all I had to forgive her. I had to forgive her for the lies that she told about me. I had to forgive her for all the snares that she tried to set up for me. I had to forgive her for how she tried to turn other family members against me. I had to forgive her for many things. And, honestly, I still must forgive her daily!

I had to forgive her without her ever saying, "I'm sorry."

I had to forgive her just like Christ had forgiven me of my failures and my faults. In the frailty of my flesh, and the sin in my marrow, He forgave me. He forgave me despite the people that I had hurt. He forgave me despite the ways that I had lived my life to disprove Him (not really understanding the magnitude of who He actually was). Christ forgave me and loved me in all my unworthiness, so who am I to hold back my forgiveness from someone who has shunned me and done me wrong? Just as forgiveness was multiplied unto me, so must I measure it out to those in need of it.

It has not been an easy task—not at all—but my freedom is worth it.

To my aunt—because I'm 95% sure that you'll read this—*I love you and I forgive you. I'm praying that you receive all that God has to offer you (salvation, healing, deliverance, the whole nine). I forgive you for all the times that you told me that I would never make anything of myself. I forgive you for all the times that you made me feel worthless and unwanted. I forgive you for all the times that you tried to gaslight me and make me feel like I was being too sensitive. I forgive you for all the lies that you've spread about me in our family, and how you continually try to turn people against me. I forgive you for all the times that you've slandered my name (in private and in public). I forgive you for all the times that you've betrayed and manipulated my trust. I forgive you for trying to make me the fall person for many of your actions (on many different occasions). And lastly, I forgive you for every threat that you've ever made on my life or will make.*

I forgive you—and I mean that.

Healing Family Ties

A more subtle part of my forgiving phase was to work through and release the resentment that I had toward the members of my family that, I believed, didn't try hard enough to keep in contact with me after my mother had passed. I had passive-aggressive anger stored up in me for years and a huge chip on my shoulder as it related to family. In my heart, I taxed them for some of the pain that I experienced in my youth, because I rationalized that a healthy escape from depression or lack of affirmation would have saved me from the drug addiction or promiscuity. I reasoned that if I had a healthy relationship with those family members, maybe I would have felt safer and more valuable in life and less like a throwaway. If only I could have kept in contact with my brothers. If only I had been closer to my mother's side of the family after her passing. If only my uncles would have learned more about me before they all passed. If only, if only, if only.

But the truth was, I had romanticized what "family" should look like so much over the years that my expectations of my family were truly unattainable. There is no perfect family, but that's what I was chasing and what I expected my family to be. There are no perfect endings where everything works out in the way that one thinks it should end, and one never has to compromise. That is the hard truth that many victims of trauma have trouble coming to terms with. Not only does the world not owe you, but people aren't going to bow to your standards of how you think they should act just because you've been hurt before. And their refusal to bow to your wounds does not mean that they don't love you! Sure, it's important to have honest conversations about unmet expectations that may have hurt you or areas of your relationship that you feel can be improved upon. That's a normal (and necessary) part of the healing and reconciliation process. But you must be able, at the end of the day, to see your family members as human beings with their own story lines and struggles and trauma themselves—just like you.

I had to give my family a chance to be my family without expecting them to conform to the mold of my expectations! They were people too! And just like I expected them to take me as I am and learn the woman that I am now, I had to do the same with them. Though the process of reconciliation often goes slowly, it's worth the extra effort that it takes to rebuild familial ties where they have broken down (for whatever reason). Whether that meant asking more questions of the relatives that I knew or reconciling with relatives that I'm not close with, each renewed connection is a thread that draws the pieces of my familial tapestry closer and closer together. Revealing the quilt of my natural existence, generational fabrics worn and torn by life's woes and lives lost, a myriad of colors and textures and textiles, all forming together to create the handmade quilt that is me. I must honor the presence of every contributor to that quilt, whether they knitted a larger section of my life or just hemmed the corner, they were there. This is the quilt that I will pass down to my children one day for them to add their own squares and life experiences. And I pray that in the midst of them examining the generational archive of each stitch, they can see the beauty of the entire piece, and not only focus on why certain squares required more stitching and mending.

That's what I used to do. I would examine the tapestry of my heritage and become sad that there were so many places that were torn. I would mourn the family that I believed that I "should have" and shun the very family that I did have. All I could see were flaws. All that I could see was hardship, tragedy, and death all throughout our family line. All that I could see was generational hurt and depression. But amid my griping, God gave me a mature revelation.

> *I was holding my family to a standard that even I couldn't reach — perfection.*

I was holding my family to a standard that even I couldn't reach — perfection. I needed perfection, though I was desperately flawed. I was expecting the Brady Bunch but bringing the Adams family. In doing that, I caused more hurt and distance than there already was on both sides of my family. Now, I'm in a place where God has taught me compassion and the power of familial reconciliation, especially in the wake of all the family that I've lost. God taught me that, though there may be many branches of my family tree that are broken, through reconciliation by His strength, those branches can be grafted back on, making the overall family tree healthier and fuller. What branch falls from a tree and then despises the tree for its existence? And what happens to that branch after it has fallen? It begins to decompose slowly and gets eaten by the dwellers of the ground—insects and animals. It becomes trampled under the foot of passersby or thrown haphazardly for another's entertainment. It may become a chew toy for a canine or a weapon for someone evil. That is what happens to a fallen branch until it withers away, in bits and pieces, returning to the dust from whence it came. I was that branch that was misused and destitute. But God is doing a mighty work in allowing forgiveness and compassion into my heart, grafting me again within the branches of my family tree, and allowing us all to bear fruit there.

Chapter 6: Casting Down the Old

Though I had experienced great forgiveness and executed great forgiveness to others, there was still much work to be done. The forgiveness of my sins and the sins of others wasn't enough to get me into Heaven or allow me to live a full life of peace. I had to continually walk out the Truth of the Gospel of Jesus every day of my life for those things to occur. That took faith, grace, and the enlightenment of God to even understand. To do this, I had to forfeit my default settings and coping mechanisms and submit every aspect of my life to Christ. If I was going to let Christ define me, then I had to take the pen out of the hands of the trauma that was writing every detail of my future. I had to make every default setting that I had adapted to deal with hurt, anger or apathy bow down before the will of God for my life. It wasn't fruitful to bathe my wounds in liquor, because after the blackout was over, I would still have to face the same pain again. It wasn't fruitful to find my worth in my ability to gratify another person sexually because sex did nothing for my soul and surely didn't guarantee the love that I was so desperately seeking. I was still left empty after the moment had peaked and passed. I needed to anchor myself in something that was real and that would give me true healing for the real issues that I dealt with daily. And that's why transformation in Christ happens day-by-day. So that every opposing challenge or innate issue that you face on any given day can be overcome and conquered, in the moment, by the Word and power of God. Living the life of a new creature would have to happen little-by-little, one decision after the other to serve God (and not myself). Day-by-day and stage-by-stage is how God orchestrated (and is yet orchestrating) my healing process from deep wounds and unhealthy vices.

Understanding Addiction

Since the age of fourteen, I had drowned my sorrows in liquor. It was a learned behavior that I felt would help me to cope just as I had seen it "help" others. But the problem with that method was that alcohol soon became one of my many ways to deflect from my pain instead of addressing it. Alcohol gave me relief, if only for a night, but came with physical and emotional consequences that would follow me in the morning. Truth be told, I didn't even need to drink alcohol to drown my pain. I drowned in my pain even when I was sober. Waves of depression would crash over me as the reality of my wounds pulled me deeper into a bottomless abyss. But it was there that He threw out a life raft and dared me to hold on to His Word, for dear life. Just like He had challenged me to forgive others while I was hurting, He was now challenging me to walk the largest faith walk of my life—facing the years of pain that I had so avidly tried to erase from my memory. He wanted to know if I would step out onto the water with Him, lock my eyes with His as we tread on the oceans that had threatened to swallow me whole. He challenged me to seek freedom from the oppression of my past and to look forward with a new hope of healing and health in my heart. He challenged me to grow. and with shaking knees and sweaty palms, I accepted the challenge.

Today is the day that I become proactive about my healing. I choose to read the Bible more and learn about this God that I'm serving. I choose to fast and pray more (because I have really been failing in that area). Most importantly though, I choose to heal. Whatever process God must use for this healing journey to be fulfilled I welcome with open arms. I know that I desperately need to be whole again. I've been through so much and have so many horrible memories—so much violence, so much pain. God has done an amazing job helping me to see myself in a different light and healing much of the pain and hatred that I felt against myself and others. He has brought me a long way from where I was, BUT I know that the journey is not over yet.

Scripture of the Day: John 5:6
"Wilt thou be made whole?"

Journal entry, Age 24

I had met The Healer and had no excuse for holding on to the pain. I had to own the effects of my trauma and stop allowing it to own me. All I had ever known of myself was the tremendous mound of broken pieces that I lugged around with me year after year. All that flooded my ears were the echoes of every negative thing that had ever been spoken over me. That is a key factor to why I drank so much. I couldn't handle the weight of always feeling like an imposter, secretly suffering, and just trying to save face. And so, I asked God to help me peel the dead layers of scar tissue off my heart and my mind and renew the fresh flesh underneath. I asked Him to transform me. Everything that didn't serve me well and everything that hindered me from pressing forward had to go. The vices that allowed me to survive in past seasons could no longer serve me

> " *I had met The Healer and had no excuse for holding on to the pain.*

in the seasons to come and it was time for them to go their way. I had to get to the root of why I indulged in what I indulged in. I had to uncover the dirt and the muck and let God get down to the root of my issues so that He could heal me there. You can't just chop down a tree and expect it not to grow again without digging a little deeper under the soil. You must pull up all those roots, however big or however small, and haul the entire stump away.

Mending the Effects of Childhood Trauma

As crazy as it may sound, I didn't even realize how much my childhood had affected my adult life. I unknowingly perceived and received the world through lenses warped by the weight of my past trauma. When someone gave me constructive criticism, I let it slide deep into my soul and validate the notion that I was flawed and worthless. I would feel uncomfortable when I received compliments because I couldn't understand how people could see value in the woman that barely valued herself. I characterized myself as shy when I was really struggling with social anxiety, constantly battling with deep feelings of insecurity and inadequacy. I believed that I couldn't trust anyone. I was deathly afraid of conflict, even in the slightest degree, whether real or imagined. Even if settling meant sacrificing my wants, needs, and comfortability in the process, I did it just to "keep the peace." These were default natures that were still in toxically engrained in the foundation of who I was mentally and emotionally. These were roots that needed to be uncovered, examined, and checked into the chipper.

> *I recently watched a video that described a complex PTSD response called "fawning." It is a response that forces a person being faced with confrontation to swallow their emotions and be passive, doing everything in their power to please their aggressor in an effort to lessen the impact or*

trauma. I am just now realizing, for the very first time, that there is a name for the feeling that I've often felt when faced with instances of real or imagined confrontation. That feeling that causes me to panic and revert to a place of wounded nostalgia, employing my oldest survival tactic to avoid blowing a flame into a wildfire.

I fawn.

This is the steel trap that has held my voice victim all these years. This is why I swallow my pain so uncomfortably. Therefore, I've always 'gone along to get along.' Just like that grown elephant who still believes that the stick in the ground can hold it down, when faced with any measure of confrontation, I shrink, emotionally retreat, and I fawn.

"The Delicate Fawn"

These are all the knots in my heart that God wanted to unravel. Now, I want to make it clear that I had truly forgiven the people that caused me the pain that I had to heal from. I forgave (and still forgive) them for how they've treated me or what they did to me. However, if the truth be told, after the act of forgiveness, we are still left to tend to the wounds that were caused by the offending act. My forgiveness says that I hold no more charge against others for what they've done, but my reality says that I still have the scars and raw bruises to show for it. That concept took a very long time for me to fully grasp, but I believe that it was a crucial lesson that I had to learn. Though the initial act of forgiveness is freeing, I must pursue total healing to maintain that freedom. For me, healing from feeling voiceless came with the knowledge and understanding that my voice was valid and beautiful and necessary for the generation that I stand in. My voice has worth and merit and weight because God has put a word in my mouth. It is the voice that speaks softly to others who have experienced unspeakable trauma and says, "Your life matters and can be beautiful." It is the voice that sings out during the darkness until the sun begins to rise and then sings a fresh tune to the morning dew. It is the voice that speaks with love, grace, and compassion. It is the voice that God, so specifically, fine-tuned just for me. Little did I know that in that "work" that God had called me to do lay the keys to my vocal freedom. He asked me, once again, to step out onto the water with him and trust Him as He led me into the next season of my very vocal purpose—preaching, teaching and evangelizing for the Kingdom of God. While the enemy of my soul and the trials of life had done everything to shut my mouth and paralyze my vocal cords, God had already spoken a purpose in me that would open my mouth and speak the greatest words that the world could ever hear, "There is hope and there is healing in the cross."

I'm beginning to realize why I've faced as many attacks as I have in my life. It was the enemy's attempt at silencing the greatest weapon that God has ever given to me—my voice. Some people forced me to shut my mouth while the stain of devastating trauma convinced me that I had nothing worthy to say. Depression caused me to internalize every agony, and apathy caused me to force my feelings down deeply. It was the only way that I knew to survive—Keep my head low, keep my mouth shut, swallow adverse emotion, and smile falsely with gritting teeth.

I learned to keep what was left of my voice under guarded lock and key, labeled, "Incredibly fragile. Handle with care." I cradled my voice like a baby and deemed it the only sense of self that I had left that was truly mine. I held that little voice tightly to my chest, curling my back over it so that it couldn't be blinded by the heat of the sun; hovering over it like an anxious mother over her first child. I held it so tightly though, that I ultimately stunted its growth. My voice never got the opportunity to operate effectively, learning to articulate itself and stand up on its own two feet. I never gave it the opportunity to reinforce what my heart felt and speak up when my body felt uncomfortable. And now finally, I have opened my hands to see the little voice box that I had been guarding and hoarding all to myself. And there my voice laid, limp with fingerprints about its neck and winded lungs still gasping for air.

I had gripped it so tightly, out of fear and anxiety, that I had inadvertently helped to silence it.

I had unknowingly crushed my already crippled voice.

But I choose THIS day to allow God to breathe the breath of life back into my vocal cords. I choose today to open my mind and my heart to the weighty worth of the voice that God has given me. Though its legs may be shaky, and its strength may be weak, I am walking in faith trusting that God will heal my voice as I go. The strength of my voice, backed by Christ's supernatural power, may scare even me, but I will cry as loud as my God allows. It is time for the caged bird to hear the beauty of her song against the winds of open air.

It is time for me to SING.

"Finding the Strength of My Voice"

And from that day forward, I made a commitment to be more vocal and to speak more intentionally about my boundaries and my feelings. The old Fetima had passed and the new Fetima walked with great power and confidence and authority. I would no longer allow the voices of my past, be it the voices of people or the echoes of anxiety, dictate to me what my life would be. I would speak back the Word of God and decree the promises that God had spoken over me to affirm myself as a beloved child of the most-High God!

I began to speak Biblical declarations over myself often. I would pour myself over the Word of God, devouring it like I hadn't eaten in a thousand years, allowing God to minister personal messages to me through the ancient text. I saw my life and my story unfolding as I read through the stories of the Bible. I was Eve, a woman whose innocence was corrupted by naivety, desire, and curiosity. I was the fallen woman, but God had already planned—from the beginning—that I would be victorious in the end. I was Esther, a woman called out from her people and destined to change the course of their very future as she walked in the anointing of God. I was David, the young child whom everyone overlooked that God had called to royalty in Him. He would show me, day-by-day, the smooth stones of His Word that I would hurl at the heads of every giant that threatened to curse my bloodline. I was the woman with the issue of blood, beckoning Jesus and thronging the crowd, even dragging myself across the floor and the feet of others to receive my healing from the Lord. I was the man that was blind from birth, a person deemed disabled and incapable, only so that God could heal me of my wounds and reveal His glory through my life. I was Mary Magdalene, a woman searching for love and affirmation in all the wrong places, which received no condemnation from her Christ. I was Joseph, who was betrayed by family for seeing visions of a blessed and ordained future, but God raised me up and allowed me to issue forgiveness to the very family that would rather have seen me die in a bottomless pit. I was Gideon—the one who was the self-proclaimed "least" in my house—but God called me a mighty woman of valor and told me that He was with me.

I am not my feelings, sexual prowess, or sexual desires. I am not defined by depression or anxiety or my fears. I am not the pulp that life chewed up and spit out. I am not the sum of my brokenness and that only. I am the woman who God sat down beside and spoke purpose to. I am the woman that God has called to knock down the idols of my kinsman and raise up an altar in His name, changing the future course of every seed that will come from me. Giving hope to every member of my family that will hear the gospel and heed the Word of God. I am the woman that God works miracles in and works miracles through. I am the woman that God has chosen to command armies that will crush the work of every enemy that has tried to pillage my village time and time again.

I am a woman of worth. I am a woman of divine purpose that will bless my family for every generation to come until the Lord comes back to retrieve us. I am the mother of nations, sowing nurturing seeds of faith and righteousness in the soil of every heart that will come from me, even before it forms. I speak prosperity over my bloodline. I speak healing over every generation of my family, either present or future. I speak dominion over every demon that has tortured our bloodline for generations and crush them under my feet by the might of Jesus Christ. I am the gatekeeper of my home and my life, with God being my shield and my buckler!

> *I am a woman of worth.*
> *I am the warrior that runs to meet the fight instead of cowering in the dark!*

I am the warrior that runs to meet the fight instead of cowering in the dark!

I am more than a conqueror.

The lies that I had believed of myself could defeat me no more, but I still had to manage the sinful desires of my members. I had learned the beauty of my identity in Christ but now I had to walk in the disciplines of it. Every person that I identified with in the Bible was only blessed when they surrendered all their lives to God. I couldn't walk in identity and live in impurity. God wasn't going to bless that. And just to make these clear, it wasn't about being perfect or doing everything right at every single opportunity. It was about having a heart that was broken for the things that broke God's heart and living a life that was consistently submitted to Him for His approval. It's just like having to follow the clauses of a will or trust fund—if you don't follow the rules, you forfeit the reward. It was as simple as that. If I wanted to hold the reins of my destiny and charge forward, God being my guide, I had to follow the rules of the track. God had given me a taste of what my life could be, and He beckoned me to come and learn more about myself in Him. He bid me to come and keep coming. He bid me to walk with Him and not grow stale. He told me that if I called to Him, that He would answer, and show me great and mighty things that I know not. And so, I let Him lead me, learning all the rules along the way.

Sexuality and Self-Worth

My knowledge of sexuality and sexual identity started with my molestation at age seven but was egged on by another childhood event later in life—pornographic dreams specifically, about women. And, for some reason, the women in my dreams would be fully grown though I was only ten years old when they started. The dreams would be lucid, allowing me to think and act on my desires just as I would in the waking world. There were no rules in those dreams, and I was able to explore whatever curiosities that I had there. But there was an aggressive sexual force that would push me in these dreams to do things that I had never seen before when I was awake. In the dreams, I was sexually aggressive, overstimulated, and seemed to know a lot more about the female anatomy than I did in real life. The women in the dreams would be passive, allowing me to do what I wanted and be very responsive to my engagement. I would awake from those dreams aroused but ashamed, wondering why they felt so real and what enjoying the dreams meant for me. Though I hid the dreams from my grandmother and everyone else, slowly but surely, the continual occurrence of such dreams started to change my perception of myself and other girls my age. I found myself sneaking glimpses of my classmates when they weren't looking and seeking out sexual or pornographic images in various forms of media (print, online and on television). True molestation had opened my body up to sexual activity, but it was the lucid dreams that caused me to crave it. I wanted to feel the arousal that I felt in the dreams while I was awake, and I chased it at every opportunity. I began dating girls in high school and had labeled myself as a full-blown bisexual by senior year—a title that I would wear proudly for a total of six years after that. Being intimate with the same sex did something to me that being with the opposite sex didn't. It fulfilled the lust of a seed that was planted in me from childhood perverting my thoughts and causing me to be confused about my identity. Slowly, I began to realize that I was not chasing women for the sake of a love for women, but because my addiction to pornography caused me to sexualize every woman that I saw. With men, I wanted relationships and marriage, but with women, all I wanted was a good time to satisfy that itch. I didn't care about their lives. I didn't care about their souls. I just lusted after their bodies and never really viewed them as whole people. I was not in right fellowship in my relationships with people, and I certainly was not in the right fellowship with God. I wasn't even in the right fellowship with myself. My worth had always been tied to my ability to be wanted and to have others be pleased with me, and this nature carried over into my sex life as well. I was completely addicted to sex and my mind (and body) had been programmed to believe that sex was the only way that I wouldn't feel empty.

But God, in His infinite wisdom and grace, knew my worth before I had ever tainted or downplayed its value. I had to ask the Savior to help me to sift through the broken shards of sexual identity, a mirror image of myself that had been shattered abuse after abuse. Who was I without sexual contact? What gauge would I have to weigh my worth in if it weren't my body?

Eve Before Fruit

> "1 I BESEECH YOU THEREFORE, BRETHREN, BY THE MERCIES OF GOD, THAT YE PRESENT YOUR BODIES A LIVING SACRIFICE, HOLY, ACCEPTABLE UNTO GOD, WHICH IS YOUR REASONABLE SERVICE. 2 AND BE NOT CONFORMED TO THIS WORLD: BUT BE YE TRANSFORMED BY THE RENEWING OF YOUR MIND, THAT YE MAY PROVE WHAT IS THAT GOOD, AND ACCEPTABLE, AND PERFECT, WILL OF GOD."—ROMANS 12:1-2 KJV

If I were going to live in the will of God, I would have to sacrifice my body to God and not to other people. Being saved from sin was not just about the baptism and Holy Ghost, but it was also (even more largely) about the life that I lived daily. I had to die every day from the temptations of my body and anything that displeased God according to His Word. I couldn't be conformed to the world and culture, which praised a woman with extensive sexual prowess and scoffed at the psychological and emotional effects of pornography. I had to allow my mind to be fully transformed by the Word and Spirit of the living God, thinking on what is good and pure and just and of good report. After all, my body was no longer my own. I had the Spirit of the living God residing inside of me, so my members were a temple, the sanctity of which could not be disturbed!

I could not wield my body like I wanted to if I was going to remain new through Christ.

Now, I'm going to be honest with you, the process of practicing abstinence was a very tough one for me. I had been addicted to sex and pornography for almost ten years by the time that I had met Christ, and both acts were heavily engrained into my daily life. I had sex to feel powerful (with women) or feel loved (with men) and watched adult movies to unwind. I was always accustomed to having my thoughts completely consumed with sexual images or desires. Sex bubbled up in my appearance and body language and in my communication with others, but I could no longer allow my sexuality to inform by eternity. I was now called to a higher calling in Christ Jesus and I had to hold myself accountable to that. I wanted to live a Christian life of integrity, so that meant that I couldn't have my cake and eat it too (my sin and His sacrifice). I had to choose. Obedience or oblivion. I had made a commitment to God and told Him that I would surrender whatever I needed to forfeit to be free and free indeed.

So, I lifted my sexuality to God, just like I had done with so many other things before and prayed that His perfect will be made manifest in my life. I had to give my old sexual identity to God, asking Him to cleanse me from all confusion and unrighteousness, reorienting my thoughts and desires to be in line with His will and His Word. I had to forfeit pre-marital sex and all of the soul ties and unrest that came with it, receiving healing for my unhealthy need to feel connected and desired. My identity could no longer be found in my sexuality because only God had the authority to tell me who I was. I had to forfeit my desires for women, because God created man and woman—emotionally, mentally, spiritually, and physically—to fit jointly together, letting no man put their union asunder. As God started shifting my perspective from myself and the world around me, I became so consumed with seeking after Him that I no longer had the same hunger for sex or for women. Now, did I still get tempted occasionally? Yes, of course.

Temptation is not the absence of deliverance, but the frailty of humanity. Because of the Adamic nature that courses through our members, temptation to sin is something that we will have to battle daily. However, through the power of prayer, fasting, and the Spirit of God, Christ can draw that nature out of you with a few passes of His hands. We are not powerless against sin, because God always provides a way of escape with the temptation. We are always given a slight pause before we err. The pause where the world momentarily stands quiet and still, and we can feel the weight of our next decision riding closely on our coattails. I had to learn to take the "outs" that God granted to me, because every missed opportunity to choose correctly gave the enemy an opportunity to bind me again in shame and condemnation. I refused to give the devil that much room in my walk with God. After a while, I began to lose the desire to watch pornography altogether. My eyes had finally been opened wide enough to see through the trap of fulfilling the lusts of my youth. The women that I took pleasure in watching were beings that God intricately crafted for divine purpose, just as He had crafted me. They were so much more than what they were doing, and as a minister of the Gospel, it was my duty to share that message of hope and wholeness and not to participate in nourishing the deeds of their flesh that were corrupting them spiritually. Those women were souls that also needed to know God and their worth. They also needed to know that there was divine purpose written into the fabric of their DNA, a purpose that God Himself is excited to make manifest in their lives. They, too, were so much more than their bodies and what their bodies could do.

We live in a world where sex and sexual expression is wildly celebrated and heavily promoted. But during all of that, God was cultivating a purity in me that would bring Him glory because of where I came from. A purity that could serve as encouragement to all who felt trapped by impurity of the mind, body, and soul. God was calling me to a purity with Him that I could boast to my husband about. And at the end of the day, that was what I truly desired at that point—a marriage to a Godly and honorable husband. I wanted consummation with marital commitment and less conjugal visits in my basement apartment. I wanted to experience God's best for me, and that included His best match for me romantically and sexually (because sex was indeed created by God). He literally created men and women to be able to come together sexually, every muscle and nerve ending neatly tucked in its proper place. I desired to make love with the man that was sent to me by the God who loves my soul. The man that would also know that, though my body does things that are pleasing, it's sexual properties or abilities do not define who I am or what I'm worth. I wanted the man that was created, by God, specifically for me. The one that I could build a life with and bear children for. The man that could love me while I was yet learning to love myself (and there was so much of myself that I was just learning to love).

A man like Ronald J. McCray.

Chapter 7: God-Ordained Love

Remember when God told me that one day, I would marry a minister? Welp, God is not a man that He should lie. As God was teaching me all these wonderful life lessons, He was lining up my path with the man that I was meant to marry. The man that He highlighted to me in a hallway of our high school, even though he was also gay at the time. Who would have thought almost ten years after God whispered that prophecy into my ears, He would allow me to meet my future face-to-face? He first noticed me while we were attending Sunday school at my cousin's (now my) church. The Sunday school teacher was discussing the story of Gideon and told us that if God were speaking to us, it would be in our best interest to heed what He says. It was in that moment that I silently prayed to God that I was now ready to accomplish this work that He had told me about before I had ever learned His name. I said, "Lord, you told me to seek You in the water and I was baptized there. You said that Your Spirit would give me power, and I have received it. I'm ready to accomplish the work." After the class had dismissed, a man walked over to me. That man was Ronald McCray.

He told me that God had spoken to him and instructed him to tell me that God has a work for me to do, and that if I pray and seek Him, He will show me what it is. My jaw hit the floor! This man

God-Ordained Love

had just spoken a phrase to me that God had been speaking to me, in the privacy of my own ears, for all my life!

How could this be true?

> **"** *This was no ordinary love—this was God ordained.*

This was my first experience in understanding that the God that spoke to me was the God of the Bible and He is speaking to every heart just like He was speaking to mine. This was a monumental moment in my faith! God had sent this word through a man that I barely knew and hadn't seen in a decade. Though we attended the same middle school and high school we never ever spoke to one another. We had all the same friend groups but were somehow never introduced. I believe that God had it that way for a reason. We were meant to meet on this side of our transformation in Christ. We were meant to meet as new creatures that had learned to love the God of our salvation and were walking out the paces of our identity in Jesus. We slowly became friends and quickly became best friends. We would talk all day long, during work and after work, soaking up each other's presence whenever we found a second to spare.

But God was brewing something in our hearts that neither one of us had expected—an unexplainable freedom of trust. Before I could shut my mouth, I had told Ron everything about myself from my fears to my scars to my deep insecurities that God was still working on. In just a few months, I had shared more with him than I had shared with friends that I had known for decades. It was like word vomit, but I felt a peace that my fragile gems would fall on good ground. Ronald then returned the favor. He told me about his struggles, his trauma, and his fears. We bonded over the brokenness, reveling in the fact that we could finally share space with a person that could empathize and not just sympathize. In many ways, we had lived the same life. We both had experienced molestation. We both had experienced rape and then promiscuity. We both carried wounds with spots that were still a little sore. We knew that this connection was not by happenstance, but by divine appointment. This was no ordinary love—this was God ordained.

Re-Learning Intimacy

Ronald is the kindest, sweetest, and most gentle man that I've ever been with. I often call him 'the ice to my fire,' and he is just that. He offers a level head when I'm feeling emotional, or a soothing tone when I'm feeling defeated and some tough talk when I'm selling myself short. He saw me in a time when I didn't know how beautiful it felt to be seen. In the moments that I wanted to hide and crawl into myself, he offered me his hand and beckoned me to stay out in the sun for just a little while longer. In the moments where my insecurities began to seep into my perception of myself and who I could be, Ron would tell me who he saw when he looked at me. A woman of worth. A beautiful, resilient woman who never stopped smiling and never stops trying. A woman who never let the love inside of her die no matter how much pain and rejection tried to snuff it out. Ron saw me as God saw me, loving me with the same heart as the One that created me. Ron didn't see me as my past. He didn't see me as my trauma. He didn't call me by scars, he called me by my name. He spoke over me a beautiful future as long as I let Christ be my guide. I think that's what I hated at first but learned to absolutely love about him. When Ron spoke about my beautiful future, he never forced himself into the picture. He never manipulated the beauty of my future to be something that could only be attained with him. He talked about me as a whole woman, completely separate from him with my own path, my own purpose, and my own mantle, and I wasn't accustomed to that. I was used to men telling me that my future would be great "with them." My happiness hinged conditionally on the success of those relationships. I had never had a man pour so much into me without requiring something in return. That's when I knew that he was a man that could love me right, like I should be loved. I had waited so long to find a man that could truly look at me and see me, bare me, with all of my scars, heart, hopes, fears, and still speak life and success and victory over me. I had found the man that saw the beauty of who God had crafted me to be.

Ron led me to deepen my relationship with God and showed me what it meant to allow God into our relationship. We prayed together. We fasted for the same causes together. And we studied the Word of God together as he asked me thought-provoking questions about what the ancient text meant for my own modern life. What I'm grateful for is that he stretched the limits of my faith before he ever even touched my body. Our lives were defined by our commitment to God and our love for each other grew even deeper as we each grew closer to Him. We both honored the other's commitment to maintain sexual purity until marriage as we both had histories of searching for love through sex. We wanted to make sure that we had an opportunity to really get to know each other outside of the lens of lust. I wanted to know his mind and he wanted to know mine. I wanted to know his dreams and he wanted to know mine. Though I was largely afraid to open my innermost emotional spaces, I felt safe with him because I saw the anointing of God in him. I heard that comforting wisdom that could only be echoed from the lips of the Father. Ron saw the same in me.

Our love blossomed quickly and felt like a whirlwind. We were completely enamored with one another. He introduced me to his love of music and gospel artist, Karen Clark Sheard; and I introduced him to my love of poetry, art, and museums. We bonded over our love of nature and water and spent many of our dates soaking in the sun and taking in the earth's natural beauty, marveling at both the creation and the Creator. I supported him in his pursuit of singing professionally, and he supported me as I stepped out into my passion for acting, writing, and producing. We pushed and promoted one another constantly, each egging on the other's growth. It wasn't too long before we started talking about marriage—not generally, but specifically about the joys of being married to one another.

I remember when Ron popped the question. I knew that a proposal was coming because we were already in premarital counseling (something that I recommend for every couple that is looking to get married). I just knew that it was going to take place on the day that it did. I was sweaty, looking plain and had no makeup on. Ron and I had just come from outreach with our church and had decided to have an "impromptu" date at National Harbor, the place where we had our very first date. He led me to the rock that we sat upon on that fateful night as we folded over laughing at ridiculous stories and poking fun at each other. I remember thinking to myself that the first date with Ron was the best date that I had ever been on because it was calculated, beautiful, hilarious and had no undertone of sexual pressure or awkwardness. It was just pure and simple, and we fell head over heels for each other immediately. So, it made perfect sense that Ron would choose that specific rock to propose on. He started by cracking a joke, flashing those beautiful dimples, and then whipped out the rock (the one on the ring)! I told him that I could shout! I felt so blessed! All that I had ever wanted was finally at my feet. Healing for my heart, strength to my soul, and now a real love for my life.

My wildest dreams and oldest prayers had finally come true.

I started to prepare immediately. If I was going to be a wife, especially the wife of a minister, I had to look the part. I had to walk the part. I had to talk the part. But most importantly, I had to do whatever I needed to do to make sure that he didn't change his mind before we made it to the altar.

Codependency Kills

Soon after the proposal, I found myself spending more time with Ron and less time with God. Running home to my living room to pray to my God after a long day became running home to call Ron and talk to him for hours instead. I became obsessed with becoming the kind of wife that Ron said that he needed—his support system, his cheerleader, his proofreader, his intercessor. I began to pray more about how to be more pleasing to Ronald than I prayed about how to be pleasing to God. I started asking God to make me all that Ron needed me to be instead of asking any more about my individual purpose. I was falling into old habits and desperately losing myself again. As a result, God began to speak new words to me that I had never heard him say before:

"*Talk to me like you talk to him.*"—as I began to pray more out of obligation than relationship.

"*I've missed you.*"—as I returned to my dedicated prayer time after missing it for months.

> *" My life was meant to be so much more than being a man's wife.*

I had become more enthralled in the future of my romantic relationship than I had been with pursuing and completing my purpose. God saved me for a purpose, and I was losing sight of that more and more as the days went by. My marriage was not just meant to be a blessing to me and Ron, but it was meant to be a beautiful, purposeful, ministry collaboration orchestrated by God. There was so much more riding on our lives and our marriage than personal validation. Our union was a part of a higher calling in Christ Jesus. And if we were to operate in that higher calling, then we had to enter our marriage with our hearts in the right posture and priorities locked on heaven.

My life was meant to be so much more than being a man's wife.

To remind me of that fact, God put my fiancé and I on pause. All at once, what was wonderful and moving so deliciously fast seemed to be turning in the opposite direction. Everyone that had supported us, began to turn on us and question us. Those that we held in high regard began to be disapproving of our plans to wed. We began to wonder what went wrong so quickly.

In Proverbs 21, the Bible talks about the heart of the king being in the hand of the Lord. This scripture talks about God's sovereignty and the strength in knowing that there is nothing that happens on this earth that God is not in control of. So in the midst of all of this sudden calamity, we sought the Lord and asked Him if it was Him changing the direction of our relationship (because at the end of the day, only His opinion is the one that mattered). God answered in the affirmative and separately told my fiancé and I to lay our relationship at His feet and leave it there. Ron and I were shocked, heartbroken, and confused. What had changed? What was God saying in this? Did He want us to call the relationship off after bringing us together? How long would this 'pause' last?

Ron and I decided to continue to do what we had always done with our relationship—allow the Lord's will to guide it and approve of it. And if God was saying that we weren't ready for marriage, then we couldn't (in good conscience) move forward with our nuptials. We certainly weren't happy with the direction that the Lord was taking us in, but we agreed that we'd rather be unhappy and make heaven than be disobedient and unsure of God's approval of us. After all, Ron had his own purpose in God to

God-Ordained Love

strive for, and he wasn't trying to mess up his blessings or future either. For me, 'the pause' caused me to go into a bit of a panic. How dare God dangle all that I've hoped for in front of me like a carrot in front of a donkey? How dare He toy with me like I hadn't been serving Him faithfully! In my heartbreak, my heart began to grow a little bit colder towards God. I started to feel less like He was my Heavenly Father and more like He was an unfair master, and I, the feeble worker under the whip. I prayed with no heart and read the Bible with an attitude. My daily devotions were held begrudgingly as I asked God to lead me to a daily study passage, I huffed and puffed while opening my Bible. One day, God laid Lamentations Chapter 3 on my heart to read. I had spent the night before crying out to God after a phone call with Ron. I was tired of pretending that I knew what I was doing and tired of waiting for answers from the God that only kept repeating the same line over and over...

"Lay it at my feet."

I knew that the Gospel of Christ was about sacrifice and dying to myself, but this type of intrusion was not what I signed up for! After Ron and I got off the phone, I broke down into tears and screamed at God, "Do you even care that I'm crying?! Could you just send another Word, or someone to comfort me? Must I drown in tears every night?! Can you just . . ." My throat had gotten clogged by that tingly, peanut butter lump that occurs when you get choked up. I could no longer speak words, only tears as I held my aching heart. It had been months with no answer, and I was losing faith that there would be an answer. I got no answer that night, so I cried myself to sleep and got up for work the next morning. That was the day that I was supposed to read Lamentations. I heard God quite clearly speak the scripture to my heart, but I was bitter because I felt that He could just as clearly speak the words that would allow me and Ron to move from our holding pattern. In my bitterness, I pretended to be too busy to read the scripture that the Lord had highlighted, and I went about my day acting as if I had never heard what He said. It was Tuesday, so there was Bible Study at my church that evening. I decided to get to church early for prayer (as I only worked 15 minutes away from my church at the time). As I began to tap into prayer, I felt the presence of God come over me and I could feel the heaviness in His voice as He said to me, "Do you not think that I have bottled up every tear? Do you not think that I have heard every prayer, even the ones that get trapped in your heart and you cannot utter? It has to be this way. I have to do it this way." The tone of God's voice sounded hurt and just a little disappointed. It reminded me of moments in scripture where God would speak to the rebellious children of Israel and remind them of His plans for them that He would prove if they only would be patient and trust Him. It reminded me of Jesus speaking to Peter when he took his eyes off of his Christ and began to sink in the depths of the stormy seas, "Oh thou of little faith, wherefore didst thou doubt?"

I heard the love in my God's voice as He reassured me of His sovereign foreknowledge of what was best for my life. The bitterness that bound my heart was melting away because I heard the compassion in the voice of my Father. He didn't have to comfort me, because He didn't owe me that, but His mercy towards me would not allow Him to see me suffer another day with no hope. As tears of gratitude began to flood my eyes, my Bishop took to the pulpit and announced the passage that he would be teaching that night. It was the book of Lamentations Chapter 3! I almost folded over in my seat. The first 19 verses of the chapter (written by Jeremiah the "Weeping Prophet") described how I had felt about God for those last few months. I felt that God had led me into darkness and not into light, that He had turned His hand against me, that He had shut out my prayers when I cried and shouted. I felt that He was, to me, a bear lying in wait. In short, He was an enemy that could care less about the brokenness of my heart. Then verses 21-25 of that same chapter caused by heart to burst wide open at God's love for me!

This I recall to my mind, therefore have I hope. It is of the Lord's mercies that we are not consumed, because His compassions fail not. They are new every morning: great is thy faithfulness. The Lord is my portion, saith my soul; therefore will I hope in Him. The Lord is good unto them that wait for Him, to the soul that seeketh Him. (KJV)

God had been trying to comfort my heart all day, but I was too stubborn to hear Him! God only wanted to give me what I asked for, which was His absolute best for me. He knew that if I walked into a marriage, solely seeking validation from my husband only, I would lose grips on the powerful woman that He had created me to be and I would have been swallowed up by whatever woman that I thought my husband wanted me to be! That is why we needed a break (at least on my side)! A machine only functions like it should if every gear is in its proper place! I couldn't go into a new level of relationship still clinging onto old ideals and habits. God had to refocus me because the purpose that He placed in me was too powerful to let die (and I thank Him greatly for that). The interesting thing is, while I was worried about becoming the woman that Ron wanted me to be, the only woman that he wanted me to be was the woman that God called me to be! He didn't want a subservient wife that only did what he liked when he liked it. He wanted to marry a woman walking in her purpose! Ironically enough, that was one of the things that first attracted him to me — my love for God and my pursuit of His will for me. So not only would I have been killing the purpose that God had placed in me, but I would have also been selling my husband short of the woman that he first fell in love with. I would have changed for the worst and mishandled the relationship with my God and my man.

We Weddy

There were 16 months in between the time that Ron proposed to me and the moment that God allowed us to move forward into marriage. Talk about a faith walk! We stayed together throughout that entire gray area of our relationship because neither of us believed that God wanted us to separate. And God didn't desire for us to separate, He only wanted us to grow in Him that we might be stronger when we came together. After all, marriage is the union of two whole people becoming one flesh, not two half hearts becoming one mess. God had some work to do in and through us before we were able to be united. It was our first wilderness walk as a serious couple, but certainly was not our last.

Our wedding was beautiful and more wonderful than I ever could have imagined. Not because of the decorations, though they were spectacular. Not because of my dress or bouquet, though they both were grand. But, because I knew with a surety, that I was marrying the man that God had set aside specifically for me. There were no wedding jitters or high stress moments on that day. Peace and contentment had followed me all that morning as I got ready, and I was convinced that as long as Ron showed up to the altar, everything would be perfect. We could have been married in an empty room and I still would have been overjoyed. I still had moments where I wished that my parents, grandmothers or paternal uncles could have been in attendance, but my family and friends made it so that I didn't feel lonely or without support. November 7th was a beautiful day, and it will never be the same.

Ron and I were already very active in our church and our marriage only intensified that service to our local ministry. We held offices on the Young People's staff, acted in our church's Sunday school plays (I even wrote and collaborated on a few), we were on the baptismal committee, in the Bishop's choir and were mentors in the Youth Training Ministry. I, in my zeal to serve in the house of

God, even added Senior High Sunday School teacher and Chaplain of the Ministers and Deacons Wives Alliance to my list of billets held. We also were both active ministers, teaching and preaching wherever we were asked to speak. We were doing a lot to aid in the building and supporting of God's kingdom through our church. However, as much as it seemed like our lives were fully consumed in God's purpose for us, deep in my heart, I felt an inkling that I had barely scratched the surface of God's true purpose for me. God confirmed this to me during prayer one evening, showing me a vision of how all the gifts and talents that He had placed in me laid at different stages of dormancy. Freezing over like rosebuds caught in an unseasoned winter's frost. I was serving faithfully in church while avoiding the pursuit of the parts of God's plans that stretched me the furthest. God would show me how I was meant to lead conferences of dozens and even hundreds of women, and I would shy my face and cross my ankles. He would show me how I was meant to write numerous books and plays and study guides, and I would close my eyes and cover my ears, convincing myself that he surely had me mixed up with someone else. I was content in just being saved, but God had placed a special word in my mouth for the world to hear.

There is something so defiant and persistent about the will of God for His children. It will pop up in your communication with others and God might nudge you in your spirit as a little reminder of His presence. It may be displayed in something that you watch on television or social media with God giving you an ever so gentle tug on your heart and reminding you of your verbal commitment to Him. And just when you try to close your eyes and rest from the reminders of the day, purpose pops up in your dreams and greets you in the morning. I can say with full assurance that God has a specific plan for every person on this earth that He desires to work through them. But to walk in that purpose fully, you must be willing to sacrifice your version of yourself—with your frailties and inabilities—and adorn the mantle that God had placed over your shoulders for such a time as this. I found myself retreating when I realized that God was calling me to even greater heights outside of the four walls of my church. He wanted me to go out and share my story of deliverance, freedom, and healing in Christ raw and real so that others might comprehend the length and the depth and breadth of God. Though I would have loved to leave my past trauma buried, God intended to use it for the purpose of furthering His message of the Kingdom of Heaven, and the reality of hell. The ministry that God has placed in me will not allow me to settle for being a passive (albeit faithful) church member in the pews.

As far as my ministry goes, the writing of this book was the largest part of its inception. Outside of the conferences, conventions, and interviews and that my husband and I have shared at, this book is what truly holds the seeds that will bring forth the fruit of the ministry that God has placed in me. This ministry that God has crafted for me was written in the story of my life long before I had ever experienced trauma or even breathed my first breath. I had to go through the drama and the tragedy to know Jesus as not just Savior but healer and deliverer. How could I know Him as a Healer if I had never been afflicted with pain or illness? How could I know Him as a strong deliverer if I had never been bound by addiction or the yoke of sin? It almost reminds me of the story of the blind man in John Chapter 9. This man had been blind since birth, for the sole purpose of God renewing His sight and proving that He could work the miraculous. Was life likely difficult for the blind man as he grew up? I'm sure that it was, often. No doubt he found his own ways to cope with his lack of sight—maybe using a walking stick to get around safely or listening to the echoes in a room to understand its depth. I'm sure that his ways of living with what afflicted him worked just fine for him in the moment. But while he had learned to make it by in his condition, God had already made plans to heal him long before he was ever born blind.

God-Ordained Love

God took the time out of His day to work a miracle in an ordinary man's life that would open his eyes to new colors and revelations that he had never seen or experienced before. Can you imagine how it must have felt to experience the world with freshly opened eyes? That blind man may have known that the sky existed, but he would have never seen the beautiful, bright blue hue that it was stained with. He may have known that water was wet, but he would have never seen the clarity of diamond clear water being reflected by the light of the sun. And the most beautiful thing that I can imagine that formerly blind man seeing is the face of Jesus, the Eternal God in flesh, that had healed him. Imagine looking directly into the eyes of your Savior mere moments after He had lifted the veil from yours.

That is the encounter that I had with Jesus Christ. And just like that man had to struggle in his life so that the glory of God could be revealed, so have I made peace with the fact that all of my brokenness occurred for the very same reason. What Satan meant for evil, to destroy me, God has turned around for my good, giving me new life and new destiny! If the point of all my years of tears and shame and heartache was to let the pages of this book sing a song of rejuvenating praise unto Christ, then it was all well worth it. If only a handful of people read this book and are encouraged to make Christ their Lord and Savior, allowing Him to transform them through the new birth experience (Acts 2:38, John 3:3-5) then all of my life's labor was not in vain. It was only birthing pains to greater purpose. My purpose is to let the light of God shine so brightly through the darkest parts of my past that all those that are living that pain can know that there is hope. Jesus is that hope. He is trustworthy and loves you more than any man or woman or even family member ever could. No

> " *He wants to heal your heart and rid you of the sin that separates you from Him.*

matter what you've done or where you've been, God is still calling to you now and beckoning you to come. He is knocking on the door of your heart, asking to come inside so that He can shake your world up and show you the tremendous power of His might and purpose for you. You are so much more than your body, your temptations, your flaws, or your pain. Let God give you beauty for your ashes. You don't have to sit in that soot any longer. Let God give you the garment of praise for the spirit of heaviness. It has weighed down your shoulders for far too long. Let God give you the oil of joy for your mourning. Weeping only endures for a night with the Lord. He wants to heal your heart and rid you of the sin that separates you from Him. We all need Jesus—from the nicest humanitarian to the vilest offender—He died and rose again for us all.

Chapter 8: Life Now and Later

As I write this book, Ron and I have been together for just about seven years and married for five. I honestly could not be happier or feel more fulfilled than I do now. My husband and I now travel the country (physically) and the world (virtually and through media) sharing our testimonies of God's deliverance and healing power. We share how God orchestrated our love story from the very beginning, bringing together two hearts with the same broken pieces and mending them both anew. We share how the transformative power of the Gospel has cleansed us from sin, restoring every natural affection and removing the taste for any temptation that displeases God. We are not perfect, but we strive to be perfected daily, understanding that we are living testimonies of the supernatural power of God in the earth. He has connected us together, two very broken people, and mended us together as one flesh healing flesh.

We have a beautiful son named Alexander (Defender of Men) Nehemiah (Comfort of God) McCray. He is named "comfort of God" because he is God's comforting rainbow baby to us after the loss of our first son—but that's a topic for another book. This son was also prophesied to me by God, right after I had my first encounter with Ron at church. I went back to my seat after talking with Ron about "the work" that God had for me to do, and I immediately looked to God and began to pray. As I prayed, God began to speak and tell me that He was going to give me a son. A son that would be a powerful minister and asset to the Kingdom of God. A son that would face many challenges and demonic attacks but is marked by a high calling in Christ Jesus and will prevail. God had instructed me to keep myself sexually pure and told me that He would bless me with the man that was meant to be that promised child's father. He said that my child's father would be a true seeker of Him (and that Ron is), and that we would live out our days together. I say all that to say this: God knows the plans that He has for you and only you can deny yourself access to those plans. God will chase you, because of His love and compassion for you, but it is up to you to choose Him and serve Him with your whole heart. It is worth the sacrifice to get to know God and allow Him to unfold your future before you. It is a blessing to serve a God that cares enough about you to sacrifice Himself in the bloodiest way possible to eradicate everything that separates you from Him. God wants a relationship with you that will last from now until eternity. Will you give Jesus a try?

Let Him stir up the generations of your bloodline and start a new thing in you and your children. Let Him wipe away every tear that drowns your voice and keeps you silent. Let Him light the way to spiritual peace and freedom through your life.

> **"** *God wants a relationship with you that will last from now until eternity. Will you give Jesus a try?*

I have shared my story of learning and loving God through some of the hardest trials of my life. He is real and He does speak, you just have to be in position to hear Him clearly. My final question to you is this…

"Wilt thou be made whole?"

Scripture Glossary
(in order of reference)

Better is the end of a thing — Ecclesiastes 7:8

Eve tempted in Eden — Genesis 3

You shall bruise his heal, but He shall bruise your head — Genesis 3:15

Repent, every one of you — Acts 2:38

You must be born again — John 3:3-5

Baptizing in Jesus Name — Matthew 29:19, Acts 4:12

Buried in baptism — Colossians 2:12

I will not leave you comfortless (as orphans) — John 14:18

I know the plans that I have for you — Jeremiah 29:11

The hairs on your head are numbered — Luke 12:7

Knit together in your mother's womb — Psalms 139:19

God spoke the world into existence — Psalms 33:6

The Holy Ghost gives you power — Acts 1:8

The Holy Spirit speaks prayers that you can't utter — Romans 8:26

Rivers of living water — John 7:38

Sealed until the day of redemption — Ephesians 4:30

Sheltering under God's shadow/arrows by noon day — Psalms 91: 1-2

Scripture Glossary

God collects every tear — Psalms 56:8

Garment of praise for spirit of heaviness — Isaiah 61:3

Stony heart/heart of flesh — Ezekiel 36:26

I won't leave until you bless me — Gen 32:26-30

Love your enemies/pray for your persecutors — Matthew 5:44

Give without expectation of receipt — Luke 6:35

Forgive 70x7 — Matt 18:21-22

If you don't forgive others, God won't forgive you — Matthew 6:14-15

God will never leave you nor forsake you — Deuteronomy 31:6

God hasn't given us fear, but power — 2 Timothy 1:7

Nothing new under the sun — Ecclesiastes 1:9

The story of Esther — Esther 1-10

David and smooth stones — 1 Samuel 17:40

Bleeding woman healed by Jesus — Luke 8:43-48

Blind man healed by Jesus — John 9:1-12

Mary Magdalene not condemned — John 8:11

Joseph sharing his dream and forgives — Genesis 37:1-10, Genesis 50:15-21

Gideon, mighty warrior — Judges 6:11-15

Call to me and I will answer — Jeremiah 33:3

Your Body is a living sacrifice — Romans 12:1-2

Think on these things — Philippians 4:8

Same-sex intimacy — Romans 1:26-27

Eve Before Fruit

What God has joined together — Mark 10:9

Every temptation has a way of escape — 1 Corinthians 10:13

God is not a man that He should lie — Numbers 23:19

Heart of the king in God's hands — Proverbs 21:1

Oh, thou of little faith, wherefore didst thou doubt? — Matthew 14:33

Breadth and depth and length of God — Ephesians 3:18

Blind man healed by Jesus — John 9:1-12

Jesus is God in the flesh — Colossians 2:9, John 10:30

What was meant for evil is turned to good — Genesis 50:20

Weeping endures for a night — Psalms 30:5

Wilt thou be made whole? — John 5:6

Author's Bio

Fetima McCray, is a wife, mother, entrepreneur, speaker, author, visionary, preacher, and minister of God. She is a pioneer for encouraging and leading those who are in search of their identity, to do so through Christ alone. Her passion for inspiring and investing in those around her to see their full worth and potential through God, has led her to have a powerful and global impact.

Fetima is the author of 'Eve Before Fruit,' chronicling her tortuous walk on her journey to redemption in Christ, now available for pre-order on her website. McCray has been featured on such media outlets as the Christian Broadcast Network, the 700 Club, Nite Line and various other radio shows, conferences, documentaries, and internet publications.

She is a minister of the Gospel of Jesus Christ under the leadership of Bishop Charles E. Johnson, attending Greater Morning Star Apostolic Ministries in Upper Marlboro, MD.

Fetima holds an associate degree in Business Administration and a bachelor's degree in Accounting. She has founded multiple businesses across varying industries, being the CEO and Principal Painter of Limon Arts, the CEO and Chief Curator at Gifts by GiftD and the Partnering Owner of McCray Books and Media.

As a passionate minister, teacher, and author, Fetima is an advocate and catalyst for living life with God-given purpose.

Whether she's sharing her testimony of becoming the woman of God that she is today—who was once orphaned—or her journey as a believer, wife, and mother; her ministry is life giving, inspiring, and educational.

Most of all, Fetima values her first ministries—her marriage and family. She has been blessed to be married to her wonderful husband, Ronald McCray, of five years. They share their miracle child, Alexander Nehemiah McCray. Together they host Transformed Life Radio and look to honor and be a model of God's love through their marriage, family, and journey as believers. Fetima continues to find joy and excitement in sharing her testimony to encourage, inspire, and uplift those to live a God honoring life.

Let's Connect!

Let's get connected!

Go to FetimaSMcCray.com or follow us on our social media pages by scanning the QR code above. We'd love to keep in touch with you!

www.ingramcontent.com/pod-product-compliance
Lightning Source LLC
Chambersburg PA
CBHW070915080526
44589CB00013B/1310